UPSIDE-DOWN
APCALYPSE

GROUNDING REVELATION
in the GOSPEL *of* PEACE

JEREMY DUNCAN

HERALD
P R E S S

Harrisonburg, Virginia

Herald Press
PO Box 866, Harrisonburg, Virginia 22803
www.HeraldPress.com

Library of Congress Cataloging-in-Publication Data
Names: Duncan, Jeremy S., author.
Title: Upside-down Apocalypse : grounding revelation in the gospel of peace
 / by Jeremy Duncan.
Description: Harrisonburg, Virginia : Herald Press, [2022] I Includes
 bibliographical references.
Identifiers: LCCN 2022009843 (print) I LCCN 2022009844 (ebook) I ISBN
 9781513810393 (paperback) I ISBN 9781513810409 (hardcover) I ISBN
 9781513810416 (ebook)
Subjects: LCSH: Bible. Revelation--Criticism, interpretation, etc. I BISAC:
 RELIGION / Christian Theology / Eschatology I RELIGION / Biblical
 Commentary / New Testament / Revelation
Classification: LCC BS2825.52 .D86 2022 (print) I LCC BS2825.52 (ebook) I
 DDC 228/.06--dc23/eng/20220325
LC record available at https://lccn.loc.gov/2022009843
LC ebook record available at https://lccn.loc.gov/2022009844

Study guides are available for many Herald Press titles at www.HeraldPress.com.

UPSIDE-DOWN APOCALYPSE
© 2022 by Herald Press, Harrisonburg, Virginia 22803. 800-245-7894. All rights reserved.
Library of Congress Control Number: 2022009843
International Standard Book Number: 978-1-5138-1039-3 (paperback);
    978-1-5138-1040-9 (hardcover); 978-1-5138-1041-6 (ebook)
Printed in United States of America

All scripture quotations, unless otherwise indicated, are taken from the *Holy Bible, New International Version*®, NIV®. Copyright ©1973, 1978, 1984, 2011 by Biblica, Inc.® Used by permission of Zondervan. All rights reserved worldwide. www.zondervan.com The "NIV" and "New International Version" are trademarks registered in the United States Patent and Trademark Office by Biblica, Inc.® Scripture quotations marked (ESV) are from the *ESV® Bible* (*The Holy Bible, English Standard Version*®), Copyright © 2001 by Crossway, a publishing ministry of Good News Publishers. Used by permission. All rights reserved. Scripture quotations marked (KJV) are taken from the *King James Version*.

Scripture quotations marked (NRSV) are from the *New Revised Standard Version Bible*, copyright © 1989, Division of Christian Education of the National Council of the Churches of Christ in the United States of America. Used by permission. All rights reserved.

26 25 24 23 22   10 9 8 7 6 5 4 3 2 1

"For too long, we've been discipled in violence, conspiracies, and fear when all along the invitation has been to wholeness and peace. A pastoral reimagining of the apocalypse through the lens of Jesus, this book will bring relief, healing, and revelation to the church. I'm grateful to Jeremy Duncan for tackling this complex topic with equal parts scholarship and grace."

SARAH BESSEY, *New York Times* bestselling author of *A Rhythm of Prayer* and *Jesus Feminist*

"Revelation is a book of prophecy that desperately needs a pastoral touch, a guide to calm our apocalyptic fears and lead us away from all the conspiracy theories and fearmongering that surround it and toward the message of hope revealed in John's message. Jeremy Duncan does exactly that as he brings his pastoral touch to bear on a book that has for so long confused and frightened so many. Drawing from a life spent in ministry, Duncan gently guides us past the monsters and wrath to reveal a message of hope that subverts our expectations at every turn. Whether the book of Revelation is something you've passionately sought to understand or have avoided at all cost, *Upside-Down Apocalypse* is a must-read, a desperately needed message of hope and peace in a world torn apart by fear and despair."

ZACK HUNT, author of *Unraptured: How End Times Theology Gets It Wrong*

"A provocative and beautiful demonstration of how the meaning of Scripture is fundamentally transformed when we read every word through the lens of Jesus crucified."

MEGHAN LARISSA GOOD, author of *The Bible Unwrapped: Making Sense of Scripture Today*

"At a time when beasts of empire continue to rampage, Jeremy Duncan shows the enduring relevance of the book of Revelation for followers of the Lamb, who calls us to pursue peace and care for our world."

J. NELSON KRAYBILL, author of *Apocalypse and Allegiance: Worship, Politics, and Devotion in the Book of Revelation*

"In *Upside-Down Apocalypse*, Jeremy Duncan shows us how John the Revelator repeatedly upends our apocalyptic expectations: We expect Jesus to return like a lion; he shows up as a lamb. We assume Jesus will conquer evil like a warrior; he enters battle already covered in his own blood. If you're troubled by pop Christianity's interpretation of Revelation, which portrays Jesus behaving like us (violent and vengeful) instead of depicting him as the Gospels do (nonviolent and merciful), then you need to read this well-researched book. I hope you'll pick up a copy, for it's high time our violent, Hollywoodized depictions of Revelation get left behind."

JASON PORTERFIELD, author of *Fight Like Jesus: How Jesus Waged Peace throughout Holy Week*

"One of the primary uses of the book of Revelation throughout church history has been to blunt the radical, nonviolent, liberating picture of the Jesus of the Gospels. In *Upside-Down Apocalypse*, Jeremy Duncan flips that script. Drawing on recent Revelation scholarship, Duncan offers an engaging, pastoral, gospel-infused reading of Revelation that is truly good news."

DAVID C. CRAMER, pastor of Keller Park Church, managing editor at the Institute of Mennonite Studies, and coauthor of *A Field Guide to Christian Nonviolence*

"Jeremy Duncan offers a fresh look at the apocalypse, challenging the typical way of understanding the violence many see throughout it. By rethinking this apocalyptic imagery, Duncan shares a vision of nonviolence that gives real hope in a world full of strife."

BETH STOVELL, professor of Old Testament at Ambrose University

UPSIDE-DOWN
APⒺCALYPSE

This book is dedicated to my partner Rachel Duncan, who agreed that it would be fun for me to write a book in my spare time.

And to the community of Commons Church, who continues to provide me the opportunity to think and create and pursue the way of Jesus alongside each of you.

Thank you.

This book was written while on the traditional territory of the Blackfoot and the people of the Treaty 7 region in Southern Alberta, which includes the Siksika, the Piikani, the Kainai, the Tsuut'ina and the Îyâhé Nakoda First Nations, including the Chiniki, Bearspaw and Wesley First Nations. These lands are also home to Métis Nation of Alberta, Region III.

CONTENTS

FOREWORD

I f only we as a society could move past that ridiculous legacy
of Christianity that longs for the end of the world!"

Like a fungal infection from public showers at the beach,
that sentence still clings to me a decade on. We were long into
a day of a successful climate justice protest. Maybe wanting to
make connections, build rapport, or show a depth of analysis,
this comment was smiled at us organizers during a meeting
by someone new to the movement. Most responded to this
odd out-of-context remark with comic side-eye and raised
eyebrows, nearly all in my direction—among the organizers
I was the token Christian. Surrounded by a sea of riot police,
this poor soul became aware that they were drowning in an
unspoken awkwardness on our social change island. I threw
them a life buoy, explaining that not only was I one of those
Jesus-loving God-botherers but I was a pastor as well as activist educator. A few laughs later we were back to the business
at hand.

Yet, dear reader, that person had a point. A point that
makes this book so necessary.

While the book of Revelation provides rich, imaginative
material for creative, Christlike, nonviolent resistance to the

destruction of God's good creation, many Christians loot this ancient literature to hasten political and ecological horror.

Instead of looking to imitate the liberating, nonviolent Messiah Jesus, many read the final book in the New Testament longing for the annihilation of all that God so loved that God gave of Godself to save.

With all the grace afforded them by metaphorical zip ties and gaffer tape from a prepper's survival kit, these conspiratorial takes, escapist revenge fantasies, and gnostic nihilisms are bound together to make road maps, ciphertexts, and timelines that undermine everything God calls us to embody in the way of Jesus.

Love of neighbor. Good news to the poor. The healing of creation. Love for enemies. Welcoming refugees. Standing with the vulnerable. All that Christ embodied and instructed is sidelined with pietistic sincerity as Christians vote, act, and desire for history to side with their end-time speculations. Most telling of all, these so-called revelations don't reveal but rather obscure Jesus of Nazareth. Jesus of the Gospels is displaced by diabolical readings of a murderous messiah who saves not with provocative, nonviolent, suffering love but like a Marvel villain wanting to make his enemies bleed. This false christ is unable to fulfill the Hebraic hope of the healing of all things and instead reflects another thing we need healing from—the image of a capricious god. Imitatio Dei becomes a dangerous doctrine when your image of God looks like an inversion of Jesus' life.

But pastor Jeremy Duncan wants to remind us what so many who talk of "end times" so often forget: God has an end in mind—the healing of all things. The transfiguration of creation. The kin[g]dom of God on earth as it is in heaven. This is what the New Testament announces has started in our Lord

Jesus and graciously invites us to join. The good news is that the ancient Hebraic hope is underway in the most surprising of ways—through Christ, and him crucified.

That's why this book is such a gift. Intellectual integrity is not a rarity. But intellectual integrity paired with pastoral humility is harder to find. To write not in the tongues of the academy but to regular people's curiosity to aid spiritual formation in Christ is a gift.

With John the Revelator, Jeremy Duncan is your trusted guide through these visions. We are living through a moment when 99 percent of the world's population labors for the hoarding of the 1 percent; a time in history when an unprecedented ecological crisis coincides with threats to democratic ideals and processes. The temptation for escapist fantasies and denial has never been greater. Nor is the need to respond to the good news of God's great reversal, the saving of creation from all domination through the upside-down apocalypse of Jesus.

May we find our place with every creature in heaven and on earth and under the earth and in the sea, and all that is in them, in singing,

> "To him who sits on the throne and to the Lamb
>   be praise and honor and glory and power,
> for ever and ever!"
> (Revelation 5:13)

Amen.

—**Jarrod McKenna**

Founding CEO of Common Grace
and co-creator of *InVerse Podcast*
and Collective

Lands of the Whadjuk Nyoongar
(Perth, Australia)

PREFACE

Another book on Revelation? I know. I know. Everyone from Isaac Newton—yes, the guy who discovered gravity—to Nicholas Cage has taken a stab at interpreting this letter, often with disastrous consequences. Revelation, it seems, gives us an opportunity to exchange the peaceful Jesus of the Gospels for one we might prefer in a jam. A Jesus more like John Wayne, perhaps.[1] After all, doesn't Revelation tell us that the Jesus of Sunday worship will one day return on a white horse, splattered Rambo-like in blood, wielding a claymore against his enemies? It's true, the writer of Revelation does employ violent imagery in all kinds of provocative ways, but to what end? To overturn the Jesus of the Gospels? To replace the Jesus of Matthew, Mark, Luke, and John with one remade in the image of John Wick? If the Jesus of our future hope bears little resemblance to the Jesus who walked through ancient Palestine, then we should at least question whom it is we really call Lord.

Of late, however, there seems to be a sort of renascence of Jesus-centered interpretation. A recapturing of Jesus as the Word of God in history that helps us make sense of the words of God in the pages of Scripture. And this is particularly helpful when it comes to Revelation. If we can assume that the writer John has encountered the same Jesus that we have in the Gospels, and has discovered no other Jesus along the way, then we can choose intentionally and deliberately to read Revelation through the lens of Jesus' life and teachings. This is what opens us up to properly understanding the nonviolent apocalypse.

This book is an attempt to do just that—to read the vision of Revelation in the light of the Jesus we know through the Gospels. Along the way we will ground ourselves in Christ as the full revelation of the divine. We will dive into the text of Revelation, both the words on the page and the subtext of apocalyptic imagery that John employs. We'll compare those images to the way Jesus uses direct nonviolent action as the social counterpart to his teachings throughout the Gospels. And we'll attempt to uncover the ways Revelation uses the apocalyptic to uncover and then subvert the violence that underpins so much of our world today.

My hope is that together we'll discover that the Jesus of Revelation is entirely consistent with the Jesus of the Gospels and how this is the true beauty of the upside-down apocalypse.

1

JESUS AT THE CENTER

This book is about the apocalypse. Not the end of the world, Mad Max apocalypse, but the apocalypse, nonetheless. The book of Revelation is a complex and haunting text that initially struggled to find its place in the Bible but has found a way to grab hold of popular imaginations in the centuries since. The pop theology of the *Left Behind* series has garnered sales of close to eighty million copies since the first book was released in 1995.[1] Revelation's inscrutable images, mysterious identities, riddles, and codes have given rise to all kinds of violent fantasies about how the world might end. At times, it even seems like Revelation can mean whatever you want it to, as long as your imagination is sufficiently apocalyptic. Which, interestingly enough, is quite a departure from the original meaning of the word from which this text derives its name.

The English title, Revelation, is far closer to the original intent than what the Greek title has morphed into. Despite the long journey *apokalupsis* has made into the English language, the term's plain meaning is simply the "uncovering of something hidden."[2] To use *apocalypse*, in the first century, was to suggest that things were about to be made clear. Ironic, then, that we have turned it into such a mystery. A word that meant "to reveal" has come to indicate the end of all things. And that's a shame because while an apocalypse is an end—an end to one imagination, an end to a vision that is incomplete—it is also always the start of something new; a more authentic way to imagine our world.

An apocalypse by nature both expands and overturns our expectations. It takes a story we thought was done and tells us two new things. First, there is more to the story, and second, the more will change everything we thought we knew.

The film *The Sixth Sense* immediately comes to mind when I think of an apocalypse. Remember that one where Bruce Willis talks to ghosts? And no, I don't believe you when you say you saw it coming, because that really was a good twist. But here's why it worked so well. When the big reveal finally arrived, and we all realized that Bruce had been a ghost all along, it made sense. The clues had been there. The truth was waiting to be uncovered, and yet our entire understanding of the film was transformed in that moment. Every scene took on new meaning, some of them entirely opposed to what we had initially assumed. It was thrilling to have our assumptions overturned. That's what an apocalypse is for—showing us what we missed, and in that, subverting our beliefs about the world.

This book in your hands is about the apocalypse, but more precisely, it is about the way God is revealed to us. First, the revealing of God in Christ that turns our imagination of the divine upside down. Jesus shows us the complete nonviolence of a God who would rather endure death than inflict it. Second is the revealing of Christ in the book of Revelation. The unveiling of Jesus' victory that turns our expectations of power upside down, replacing them with divine renewal.

All of this is more than just a question of biblical interpretation, though. There is practical importance to how we understand a book like Revelation. The lens we choose to read the Scriptures through informs our imagination of God, and our imagination of God shapes how we act in the world.

Will we take up the challenge of climate change and work to repair the damage we have done to the environment, or will we instead give in to apocalyptic fantasies of a world abandoned to despair? Will we choose to vote for a politic that seeks to lift the oppressed and addresses structural sin, or will we prefer to train ourselves to look for enemies behind every corner? Will we place our hope in a world where all nations maintain diverse identities and worship together equally, or will we choose foreign policy that dominates, exploits, and continues our colonial legacy? Will we face down global challenges with courage and solidarity, acting in our neighbor's best interest, or will we dive into speculative resignation, misinterpreting signs and symbols that hint at sinister ulterior motives? In each of these scenarios, what we believe about God will lead us to choices that either continue the story of Jesus—or betray his legacy in the world.

My contention is that Revelation, when read through the lens of the Gospels, will help us uncover the prophetic hope that saves us from nihilistic despair. The Apocalypse will reveal a God so deeply invested in the renewal of all things that the story will push us back into the world with new eyes to uncover the divine in our neighborhoods, our politics, and even the cosmos. As Jesus once said, you are the salt of the ground beneath your feet, and the light of the cosmos above your head (Matthew 5:13–14). That's the heart, and scope, of the upside-down apocalypse, but it begins by rooting our reading of Revelation in the gospel of peace.

JESUS AS APOCALYPSE

In my church community, we often use the phrase "We are completely fascinated with this complex and beautiful collection of texts we call the Bible, but we worship Jesus." That is meant to be a little provocative. Obviously, we worship Jesus. We're a Christian church, after all. But the *but* creates this point of tension or at least a point of distinction between Jesus and the text. Now, spoiler, that's not because we actually think there is a disconnect. In fact, the more I study and the more I read, the more I invest myself in the Scriptures, the more clearly I see them pointing me back to Jesus. However, we do recognize a distinction. Scripture is where we encounter Jesus. Scripture is not a replacement for Jesus.

This, however, shouldn't be a surprise for anyone who has read the New Testament. The apostle Paul tells us in Colossians that Jesus is "the image of the invisible God" (Colossians 1:15) and that in him "all the fullness of the Deity lives" (2:9). The writer of Hebrews adds that "the Son is the radiance of God's glory and the exact representation of his being" (Hebrews 1:3). Nowhere do the Scriptures speak of themselves with such impressive clarity. In fact, the more we study the Scriptures, the more we come to see the New Testament deferring to Jesus.

If we're going to read the Scriptures well, we need to read them on their terms. And even though the New Testament is written by a collection of authors addressing various contexts, two presuppositions hold these diverse texts together. First, God is love. And second, the person of Jesus is the closest we will ever come to seeing that love embodied in human history. These are the assumptions that sit behind everything we read in the New Testament, including the book of Revelation.

Now, why is that important? It's important because our presuppositions influence everything we experience.

My favorite band happens to be Pearl Jam. I came of age right at the dawn of the '90s, and the grunge scene shaped my adolescence. That has stuck with me through to today. In 2020, Pearl Jam released their eleventh studio album, *Gigaton*. I knew I loved it before I had even heard a note. Granted, I have a lot invested in Pearl Jam. I have seen them play live in every city I have lived in. I own first pressings of all their vinyl releases. Over the years, I have made my love for Pearl Jam a central part of my musical identity.

And so I stayed up until just after midnight on January 22, 2020, to listen to the first single from the forthcoming album. It was surprising, to say the least. If you have even a passing familiarity with Pearl Jam and you've heard "Dance of the Clairvoyants," you know that it was a departure from their formula. This was a bit of a moment for me. Of course I want the members of the band to grow as musicians and creatives and be fulfilled as human beings, but the song wasn't what I expected. In an era where I can stream literally any song on demand, if this hadn't been a Pearl Jam release, I undoubtedly would have moved on to something more familiar. But here I was, already in a deeply committed relationship. I had presuppositions about the value of this music—it meant something to me—so I decided to stick with it. I listened again and again, and slowly it began to grow on me. Eventually, I picked up on themes and threads to earlier work, and over time, I grew to love not just the song but the entire album. Now, did I just convince myself I loved it? Maybe. However, I genuinely believe *Gigaton* is a great album and you should definitely go buy it. But this phenomenon is what we have to understand. The trust that we bring with us into a relationship, perhaps we could even say the faith we bring with us in an encounter, shapes what we take out of the experience.

In the same way, being Christian hands us certain beliefs before we come to a book like Revelation. Are there other ways to read the book? Of course there are, just as there are many ways to listen to a new record. But suppose we have already identified ourselves with the Jesus of the Gospels. In that case, we will specifically and intentionally read Revelation while assuming that God looks like Jesus and that Jesus is the closest we will ever come to understanding divine love in human history. These convictions will compel us to look again when the text confronts us with something we don't expect.

GOD IS LOVE

I take the statement "God is love" found in 1 John 4:8 to be definitional for God. God is the source of all good and life and creativity and beauty in the universe because God is, at the core, love. For me, this is part of why the mystery of the Trinity is so essential to the Christian faith. Trinity tells us that God is an endless dance of gift and reception, a love relationship from before there was anything. God is love. And always has been.

From this we can discern that God can be merciful, or God can be angry. God can be frustrated, or God can judge. God can be just, or God can choose instead to be compassionate. Still, whatever God does, God's actions can only ever be an expression of love because that's who God is definitionally. In other words, the God we perceive in history has to be consistent with the transcendent God who has always existed as shared love from before there was time.[3] That is pretty uncontroversial.

The next question is infinitely more complicated. What does divine love look like?

Faithful people have struggled with this question for a long time, but as a Christian, as someone who puts my trust in

Jesus, I ultimately trust that the answer to that question is Jesus. The closest we will ever come to seeing divine love in the human story is Jesus. That's the point of the whole long narrative we call the Bible.

FROM THE BEGINNING

> In the beginning was the Word, and the Word was with God, and the Word was God. (John 1:1)

These are the opening words of the Gospel according to John. That word, *Word*, is *logos* in Greek. Now, *logos* means, at its most basic, "word." So the translation is sound. Still, *logos* has a complicated history, with both significance and baggage within the Greek tradition. Around 500 BCE, the philosopher Heraclitus starts using *logos* to talk about "an underlying cosmic principle of order."[4] His idea is that *logos* represents the true essence of something. Later, Plato and Aristotle add their nuances. Both seem to favor *logos* as the act of communicating our truest thoughts,[5] although both use the term in various ways. The Stoics swing back toward Heraclitus, using *logos* to describe the rational forces that control the universe.[6] However, by the time of the Neoplatonists, *logos* has become that "force that invests material objects with their shape, and form, and life."[7] Essentially, *logos* is the idea behind the thing. And this mature concept of *logos* likely has resonance for John because it reminds him of an old, old idea—the idea of wisdom.

In Proverbs, the writer speaks of wisdom.

> The LORD brought me forth as the first of his works,
>   before his deeds of old;
> I was formed long ages ago,
>   at the very beginning, when the world came to be.

When there were no watery depths, I was given birth,
  when there were no springs overflowing with water;
before the mountains were settled in place,
  before the hills, I was given birth,
before he made the world or its fields
  or any of the dust of the earth.
I was there when he set the heavens in place,
  when he marked out the horizon on the face of the deep.
(Proverbs 8:22–27)

You can see the parallels to John's poetry here. Wisdom is personified in a relationship with God. Wisdom is from before creation. And Wisdom participates in the formation of the world. Even the language of both Proverbs and John calls back to Genesis, explicitly referencing a time "in the beginning" (Genesis 1:1; John 1:1) even before there was any deep water to hover over (Genesis 1:2; Proverbs 8:24, 27). It's this idea that there is God, and then there is the creative expression of God that brings the world into being and gives it meaning. Both John's Word and Proverbs' Wisdom are playing with this idea.

However, John makes a neat connection here. In the beginning, God created the heavens and the earth, but how did God create them? God spoke. John notices that the Greek word that means "word," the very act of speaking, has a rich philosophical history that sounds a lot like the idea of wisdom he's familiar with from Hebrew thought. And so he mashes them together in one beautifully creative moment.

John is saying that the same creativity that brought the universe to life is now present to us in Jesus. Everything that God has always been—divine creativity and relationship and love—now alive in the human story. And granted, that's a big concept, hard to get our heads around, for sure. But the essence of what John is saying is that God's Wisdom that has always surrounded us—everything God has always intended to say in creation—is now speaking in Jesus. The final Word of God.

This is similar to what the writer of Hebrews expresses by saying that "in the past God spoke to our ancestors through the prophets at many times and in various ways" (Hebrews 1:1), or what Paul is getting at when he says, "God's invisible qualities—his eternal power and divine nature—have been clearly seen, being understood from what has been made" (Romans 1:20). God has always been speaking. But now God walks with us.

JESUS IS WHAT GOD LOOKS LIKE

What this means is that, for the Christian, Jesus is the final arbiter of divine love. God speaks in creation. God speaks in Scripture. But Jesus is the *Logos* of God—the idea behind the thing.

And this is why the Gospels must be the Rosetta Stone of all our Christian interpretations. Once we observed God through a glass darkly, but now we can see God's love in action. It's also why any interpretation of Revelation that departs from the Gospels or imagines a different Jesus returning to the world has lost the plot. Even Scripture can be anti-Christ if we allow it to move us away from the way of Jesus.

So what about those parts of Scripture that prick our conscience? Those problematic passages that celebrate violence or restrict the grace extended by Jesus? Those stories that we instinctively recoil from, knowing that it isn't love on display? Well, apart from abandoning them—an option I am not disposed to myself—we have two choices. We can normalize the Scriptures or we can narrativize them.

When you work with an audio recording, say for a podcast (or a Pearl Jam album), you often want to normalize the audio. This means you compress the recording by making the loud parts slightly quieter and the quiet parts slightly louder. This way, everything becomes a more comfortable volume to listen to.

We do this all the time with the Scriptures. We try to balance stories of military conquest with the nonviolent protest of Jesus. We look for the neutral points between the cultural practices of the ancient world and the boundary-expanding welcome of the early Jesus community. We try to fashion a Jesus who can at once offer forgiveness even in death (Luke 23:34), yet also return to behead those who oppose him (Revelation 19:15). These are of course completely contradictory aims, but by bringing up the volume on violence and toning down the sound of peacemaking (Matthew 5:9), we make it work.

Still, my conscience often rebels, knowing that this doesn't feel like the way of Jesus. And so, we are told, we cannot trust our feelings, only the Bible. Except that doesn't seem to be what Jesus thinks. In his Sermon on the Mount, he says, "Which of you, if your son asks for bread, will give him a stone? Or if he asks for a fish, will give him a snake? If you, then, though you are evil, know how to give good gifts to your children, how much more will your Father in heaven give good gifts to those who ask him!" (Matthew 7:9–11). Don't miss it. Jesus acknowledges the brokenness that resides in each of us, the sin that twists our perception of love. It's a genuine problem, so we should take it seriously.

However, Jesus still regards the *imago Dei*, the image of God within us, to be operative in guiding us toward the good. This "how much more than" structure was a familiar rhetorical device in Jesus' day. It was used to solidify agreement on one premise that could then build to a more important one.

But here, Jesus' argument about the nature of God starts with the premise that you and I know love when we see it. This then leads us to the more important point: God is perfectly unhindered love. Jesus assumes that our tendency toward good can be a compass for understanding the divine.

Rather than compress the Scriptures and attempt to find a neutral point between Jesus and what we know in our heart isn't loving, the alternative is to read *through* Jesus. To embrace the whole counsel of Scripture as the unfolding story that leads us to the final Word of God. This means embracing the Bible as a complex mix of perspectives and biases, cultural viewpoints, and human experiences, all shaping a divine narrative that leads to a climax. This involves reading the Scriptures as a story with peaks and valleys and dynamic range, trusting that the story is pointing us somewhere even when the particular chapter we are reading feels murky. In this way we let God whisper when God whispers. And we let God shout divine love when God speaks through Jesus.

In this approach, every word of the story is still essential—inspired, even—because every jot and tittle is part of an unfolding narrative that reveals God's love to us. And granted, the story twists and turns before it reaches a crescendo. Of course it does. That's how a good story draws us in. But in seeing Jesus as the climax of the story—the final apocalypse that reveals God—we embrace not only the words but also the tone and texture of that tale.

God is love. Love looks like Jesus. That's the story.

2

WHAT'S AN
APOCALYPSE?

There's an old idea called the perspicuity of the Scriptures. It means that the Scriptures are clear and intelligible. I believe that. Completely. After all, Jesus tells us that faith is simple. That even a child can get it. In fact, he even seems to suggest that maybe it's easier for a child at times. To love freely and imagine a world of equity, to welcome and befriend strangers and family alike—these are all ideas that seem to be steadily drummed out of us as we grow older. But to enter what Jesus calls the kingdom of heaven, an imagination of the world informed by grace and peace, this takes the simplicity of a child who trusts more easily (Matthew 18:3). I've often thought this is what Jesus has in mind when he likens faith to being born again. It's like starting all over again with eyes wide open—everything a fresh possibility.

Good news is apparent to anyone who reads. This is what we mean by perspicuity. The Scriptures point us clearly to Jesus. Jesus demonstrates divine love for us. That love rescues and transforms and invites us on a new path. And then that love awakens us to see all of human history with eyes unveiled. Perspicuity does not mean, however, that every verse or image is easy to make sense of, or simple to reconcile. It certainly does not suggest that we can understand first-century idioms without serious study. Perspicuity reassures us that we can follow the narrative, but some of the chapters are quite murky at times.

Enter Revelation. How does a book about a red dragon, a lamb covered in blood, and a beast with seven horns and ten crowns speak to the divine love we see so clearly in Jesus?

That's where the community of Christ comes in. Interpreting Revelation alone, you and I will probably come up with readings as diverse as the two of us. Add in more people, get more interpretations. But together, sharing the wisdom and insight of the larger community, the historic collection of people who have followed the way of Jesus and studied the book of Revelation, we can find our way back to the clarity of good news, even in this difficult text.

I spent a couple of years studying Revelation in grad school. I even wrote a (long, boring) thesis about it that serves as the backbone of this book. In that research, I discovered academic after scholar after mystic who saw in Revelation a vision of the peace of Christ, not in contrast to the Gospels, but in tension with the violence of the world that surrounds us. There may not be much perspicuity in Revelation, but in holding tight to the clarity of the Gospels paired with research that illuminates the context of this ancient apocalypse, I think we can see Christ clearly here as well.

This unveiling of the world was written to church communities under immense pressure—economic, social, political, and religious—and some of the people reading this letter in the first century were acutely aware of all that pressure. They saw what was happening around them, the way the empire wanted them to conform to a counterfeit version of peace. And they fought to hold on to their imagination of the peace of Christ. Others, though, didn't feel the weight at all. They didn't see it or perceive it. They didn't realize how they were being shaped by a story different from the way of Jesus. And John works creatively and deliberately to wake them up to what really was. To unveil it all to them. And maybe also to us.

REVEALING JESUS

"The revelation of Jesus Christ." That's how the letter opens. In fact, the very first word of the book of Revelation is the Greek word *apokalupsis*. Now, the reason we don't call this book Apocalypse is simply because an *apokalupsis* is not . . . an apocalypse. The English version of this word has become intractably associated with a particular genre of fiction. We hear "apocalyptic" and immediately think of zombies or nuclear fallout or, increasingly, climate disaster. The ancient Greek word *apokalupsis*, however, simply means unveiling. It is about bringing something out in the open to be seen fully. To uncover. For example, that moment in a traditional wedding when the groom lifts the veil of the bride, uncovering her face for the first time, could very literately be one of the uses of this verb in Greek. Therefore, one of the first things we must get straight before reading Revelation is the conviction that John is not hiding anything from us here. He's trying to show us something.

So then why all the bizarre images? Why not simply come out and say what you want to say? If your goal is to reveal, why write with as much obfuscation as Revelation seems to employ?

LANGUAGE GAMES

The first reason Revelation uses such provocative imagery has to do with how we use metaphors. Metaphors help us see the world in new ways, but they depend on the shared language that we already understand.

Obviously, if I speak a different language from you, it's tough to communicate. But at its most basic, language itself is a bunch of metaphors. A series of grunts and growls that we agree represent something else. Now take that a step further and assume we speak the same language. Even within that shared language, another level of agreement is needed to communicate as soon as we take a step beyond concrete ideas. You and I are navigating metaphorical space all the time, listening to and interpreting each other's images according to our shared social conventions.

For example, if I were to say to you that the Bears destroyed the Eagles, you could probably run a quick mental checklist and infer from the casual context of the comment that I was talking about a National Football League game. Even if you don't have a closetful of sports jerseys, you live in a world where those terms, in that sentence, make the most sense in the context of sports. You might be surprised to hear that Philadelphia lost the game, but you're probably not going to be alarmed about a brawl at the local zoo. Likewise, you may be aware that eagles are often used in political discourse to represent the United States, and bears to signify Russia. Still, given the offhand nature of my comment, you probably don't jump to Cold War imagery. No one needs to explain that we're talking about sports. No one jumps in to disabuse us of the zoological or geopolitical options. We simply make a series of mental calculations to determine where these images best fit in our conversation.

The thing is, we are doing this all the time, probably far more than we realize. What if this time I open a newspaper and show you a cartoon image of an exaggerated and bruised donkey, hands wrapped in leather, wearing stripes of red and white and fighting with a bloodied and frustrated elephant, tusks of ivory, draped in stars? Are we back to imagining an outbreak of violence at the zoo? Are we now living in a world of anthropomorphized animals that terrorize our cities? Unlikely. Instead, we are probably reflecting on American politics, where the Democratic Party is represented by a donkey and the Republican Party by an elephant, the stars and stripes on their respective costumes only reinforcing those nationalistic identities. The artist doesn't tell you what the images represent; she doesn't need to. In fact, if she did, it would kind of ruin the effect.

In both of these scenarios, we don't need to explain to each other what each metaphor represents. That would only get in the way of our communication. We trust that from the context of our dialogue—being part of the same cultural milieu—we both know the language game and can interpret on the fly.

The same thing is happening in Revelation. The writer employs a dizzying array of images, bombarding us with provocative metaphors, but it's not an attempt to confuse us. It's simply that the writer expects the reader to keep up with the conversation the same way we do with each other all the time.

SHIFTING IMAGES

Okay, but why not just use plain language? Perspicuity and all that. Well, this is the thing we need to understand about metaphor. Metaphors rely on shared language, but they help us see things with a fresh perspective.

Several years ago, I was able to visit the Tate Modern art museum in London, England. I had long been a fan of Mark Rothko, and I was excited to see an exhibit of his work while

I was in town. So I made my way to the museum and spent the day wandering the halls, making all kinds of discoveries, one of which was the world of Jackson Pollock. I had seen his work before and had found it a little underwhelming. Anyone can splash some paint on a canvas, I assumed. However, standing in front of *Summertime 9A*, a massive canvas that swirled with so much emotion and energy, I found myself captivated in a way I did not expect. I walked away that day with a newfound appreciation for Pollock's artistry, even if I still can't quite explain it. Somehow, those splashes of paint were an entirely different experience in a new setting.

A highlight of the museum tour was a display of Pablo Picasso's work. When I was there, they didn't have his most famous portraits on display. They did, however, have some paintings from his Blue Period, some sketches from when he began experimenting with the impressionist style, and a couple of those later cubist works he's most famous for. It was fascinating to see the progression in his art. Although Picasso is most well known for his brilliant and bizarre portraits, he was a classically trained artist who painted in several different styles before evolving into what we think of when we think of Picasso today.

Earlier in his career, Picasso painted some very notable but nonetheless traditionally recognizable works. However, in the period leading up to the First World War, he started experimenting with what would end up being called cubism. Picasso, among others, began painting portraits where all the right features were there, but it was as if they had been taken apart and then put back together in bizarre and disorienting ways. He would paint part of a face from one angle and then add another facial feature that seemed to come from a different perspective. He would then combine those elements to create something unsettling and beautiful all at the same time. Picasso felt that in trying to express the idea of a person, to really capture the essence of a subject, he had to do more than represent the person the way we perceive them with our eyes. We can see someone, but a painting could see them from multiple angles simultaneously. And maybe that was more true, more insightful, than even looking directly at them. A new way to see someone that helped us perceive what was always there.

Good art twists the world just enough to help us see what we missed.

In the same way, Revelation is not trying to hide its meaning from us by using what might seem like bizarre imagery. John uses conventional imagery that his audience would have placed within their world to help them see their world in new ways.

When Revelation says that "the woman was given the two wings of a great eagle, so that she might fly to the place prepared for her in the wilderness" (Revelation 12:14), we shouldn't be imagining a US Air Force cargo plane transporting Israeli civilians into the desert while the battle of Armageddon rages. That neither understands the cultural context of these images nor acknowledges John's efforts to help his audience see their world in new ways. When Revelation describes locusts as powerful as horses, with tails like scorpions (see 9:7–10), we will not be talking about Apache helicopters and Stinger missiles. That interpretation imposes our context on these images and assumes that we are the ones John is focused on. Neither is true, and centering ourselves is a surefire way to miss the point.

Make no mistake, John does not believe in literal dragons and beasts and very scary grasshoppers. He believes in the ability of art to illuminate the world. And that means for those of us who come along some two millennia later, in order to understand Revelation we're going to need to learn to think like art historians.

John has something to say. He wants to tell us that everything is not what we think it is. He wants to say that the empire is not the shining light it claims to be. He wants to tell us that persecution and pressure are not signs of being abandoned by God. In fact, he wants us to know that everything that opposes the peace of Jesus is simply the last gasps of evil as it tries to hold on to what it has already lost.

John is convinced that Jesus is what is really real about the world. Still, he knows that in the midst of our struggle, amid our confusion, in our fear of what may come, it is the peace of Christ that can often feel like the illusion. Theologian Walter Brueggemann uses the phrase "monopoly of imagination"[1] to describe how empire, any empire, tries to convince us that the status quo is the permanent reality. John, knowing that he is working against not just Rome but also the way empire weaves itself into the fabric of our lives, decides against tackling the theology head-on, as Paul might, and chooses instead to tell stories. He takes the world and turns things upside down. He takes ideas apart and then puts them back together in ways that challenge our assumptions, forcing us to confront new possibilities. He uses metaphor to help us see what we miss looking straight on. And he does all this in an attempt to turn the genre of apocalypse upside down.

THE PROBLEM WITH PESSIMISM

The problem with apocalypticism was its pessimism. Yes, the word itself meant "revealing." But the genre that developed around the word was the product of years of despair. For the most part, apocalyptic writers had given up on the idea of a better world and had put all their eggs in a basket they hoped

God would show up to step on. There are many apocalyptic texts from around the time of Revelation, and they are full of violent imagery because hope for change had given way to a desire for revenge. By the time of Revelation, apocalyptic longings had largely supplanted prophetic hope in the Jewish imagination.[2]

It's not hard to see why. Despite the warnings of prophets like Hosea and Amos, the northern kingdom of Israel had fallen to Assyria. The southern kingdom had fallen to Babylon in the face of alarm bells raised by prophets like Jeremiah and Habakkuk.

Sure, there were moments of reprieve. After the Persian Empire took control, they had allowed the Jewish people to rebuild a new temple, but since then, the Greeks and then Romans had controlled the land. Slowly, a hopeful imagination for repentance and return had been replaced by underground narratives of vengeance and retribution. Apocalypse was a very popular genre.

By the time John wrote his letter, that same despair had crept into a Christian community that had seen their hopes dashed as well. Jesus was executed in the early 30s CE. Since then, more than a generation had gone by, and hopes for his return were waning as well.

Early dates for the composition of Revelation would put it somewhere in the middle of the first century. An eleventh-century bishop named Theophylact explicitly claimed that John was exiled under the reign of Nero (54–68 CE).[3] There are some coded references to Nero in the image of the beast and the number 666 (we'll get there in a later chapter), and those allusions were used to support this date for the writing.

After Nero's death, stories of his return started popping up all over the empire. Tacitus even recorded someone claiming to be Nero showing up in Rome to claim the throne in 69 CE.[4] With that in mind, the image of the beast that was slain and yet lived (Revelation 13:14) probably fits better as a reference to Nero's death and the stories that sprang up afterward than as a reference to his actual reign. But that would also mean that the letter was written a little later in the first century. Granted, Nero was no friend of the Christian story, so it's not surprising that many want to place the writing of Revelation here, given its apocalyptic tone. However, another period fits with this growing pessimism. And that is the reign of Domitian.

Domitian is arguably less famous, but perhaps no less infamous, than Nero. In the early years of the Christian story, a consensus of church fathers believed Revelation to have been written under the reign of this emperor. Irenaeus argues that John wrote "towards the end of Domitian's reign,"[5] and Eusebius repeats this hypothesis in his *History of the Church*.[6] Many modern scholars agree that given Domitian's antagonistic approach to Christianity, a dating under Domitian (ca. 81–96 CE) is the most likely.[7]

Intriguingly, that image of the beast from the sea with its ties to Nero is said to have seven heads (Revelation 13:1). If Nero is taken to be that first head with the fatal wound that is healed (13:3), then counting six more emperors brings us right to Domitian. We'll take a much deeper look at Domitian in chapter 5—he was quite a character—but for now it's helpful to know that Domitian was said to have become increasingly violent in his later years,[8] particularly toward the Christian community. Even though the evidence for the systematic persecution of Christians "is sketchy at best,"[9] that doesn't mean people weren't afraid during this period. Rumors and conspiracy can be almost as bad for anxiety levels. In truth, the varied predicaments presented in the seven letters of Revelation, with some communities feeling intense persecution while others exist in relative comfort, lines up well with what we understand about the pattern of first-century persecution under Domitian—local, sporadic, and not particularly systematic.[10] However, that kind of insecurity and anxiety, that feeling of being unsure of your place in the world, perhaps that in itself is what spurred the renaissance of apocalyptic thinking that motivated John to write.

BREAKING THE RULES

John, however, is not a pessimist. He sees the power of the apocalyptic genre—the way writers skillfully take apart their world and reconstruct it with metaphors to reveal what is hidden. He understands why people are craving such stories in the midst of their despair. But John is also profoundly hopeful. God has revealed Godself completely. Divine love is on display in history. That cannot but change the world.

And it's this double subversion that makes Revelation so fascinating. It's using the genre of apocalypse to reveal what we don't see about our world—while also smuggling in the hope of Christ to undermine the cynicism that has crept into the Christian community. Apocalypses of the day often started from the assumption that the world was so wicked, it must be destroyed. Revelation says that the time has come to destroy all that destroys (11:18). And it's this turning upside down that makes all the difference.

When a book begins with "Once upon a time," your mindset shifts into a particular perspective that prepares you for what's coming. As a storyteller, I could stay within the confines of that genre and weave a tale that brings you deeper and deeper into your expectation. There is a certain charm in that—think *Beauty and the Beast*. But these stories appeal because they play within our expectations. However, I could also open with "Once upon a time" but play against the convention. Instead of a fairy tale, I could unfold a story designed to undermine the premise of "once upon a time," using that to play with your expectations—think *Shrek*. Both *Beauty and the Beast* and *Shrek* are great stories. Both use the rules of the fairy-tale genre. But one uses the rules to welcome you into a world with beasts and talking cutlery. The other uses the rules to set you up for the punch line. Either way, the stories depend on us understanding the rules of the genre.

The first word of Revelation, *Apokalupsis*, is a "once upon a time" that sets the stage for us. But everything after that is upside down. Revelation is more *Shrek* than *Beauty and the Beast*. Scholars of Revelation have long understood this phenomenon—that Revelation actively resists being boxed in to a particular genre.[11] This is a crucial part of the story, though. When a text moves back and forth between genre conventions, it creates a sort of disorienting experience, which in itself becomes part of the point.[12]

One of my favorite books, and for that matter movies, of the past decade is *Annihilation*. Without giving too much away, author Jeff VannderMeer starts with a story that feels like a reasonably classic sci-fi tale. The story then (Vannder) veers hard and fast into something more like a horror story before ultimately swinging into a surreal fantasy. It's great. You should read it. And when you're done, go and watch the film adaptation, which is very different and yet somehow retains all the genre-crossing that makes the story work. It's precisely this loss of equilibrium that hybrid texts like *Annihilation* and Revelation use to create meaning as they play with what we expect from them.[13]

To do this effectively, it's clear that the author of Revelation is very familiar with the apocalyptic tradition.[14] After all, you have to know the rules before you can break them. But John is also subverting the very premise of the genre.

SUBVERSIVE STORYTELLING

Revelation walks like an apocalypse and talks like an apocalypse, but Revelation is not your typical apocalypse. Instead, Revelation uses our apocalyptic expectations to subvert our assumptions about the world.

And this is not a strategy unfamiliar to Jesus. There's an interesting, if uncomfortable, exchange between Jesus and a Syrophoenician woman in Mark 7. This foreign woman comes and begs Jesus to heal her daughter. He responds, "First let the children"—referring to the Jewish people— "eat all they want, for it is not right to take the children's bread and toss it to the dogs"—referring to Gentiles like herself (7:27). Awkward.

Undaunted, in the next verse the woman replies, in essence, "I hear what you're saying, but respectfully, even the dogs sneak under the table to eat the children's crumbs." And Jesus says, "Okay, well played. I will heal your daughter after all. She is well."

This complex story has inspired all kinds of speculation, but to really understand the exchange, we have to remember that it is part of a larger section in Mark. In the verses immediately preceding the exchange, Jesus has just been teaching, attempting to clarify the meaning of certain traditions. Essentially, he says rituals are good, but rituals are intended to foster a sense of moral clarity within us. Lose sight of that, and we lose sight of what's truly important. To which his disciples immediately say, We don't get it. And Jesus explains again. Nothing that enters a person from the outside can defile them. Food doesn't go into your heart. It goes into your stomach. It's what comes out of a person, out of a person's heart, that tells us about them. Rituals and traditions are beautiful, but if things like theft or murder, adultery or greed, malice or deceit come out of you, what's the point? In other words, the traditions that set you apart are doing their job only if they point you back to others with more compassion and grace.

But then, in the very next set of verses, this foreign woman asks for help, and Jesus says, "Hey, we have rules about who gets what first."

And the woman says, "Sure, but you've told us that God loves everyone, and the rules are meant to remind of this."

So Jesus says, "Exactly." And then, perhaps to turning to his disciples, "See, she gets it. She's been paying attention. Do you guys see it now?"

This whole exchange is meant for the disciples. It's a bit of theater. Jesus shows them what they expect and then pulls the rug out from under them to illustrate this woman's wisdom and the graciousness of God seen through it. It's about expectation turned upside down on the disciples.

THE ANTI-APOCALYPSE

John wants to do something similar in Revelation. He knows his audience is pessimistic. He understands they are scared and looking for revenge; that's only natural given their circumstances.

And, of course, in those moments we expect God to react like us. Our Scriptures are full of our violence placed in the mouth of God. Except now we have seen God fully revealed in the person of Jesus. The apocalypse of God's true nonviolence. Pessimism and fatalism, negativity and gloom, as attractive as they are in a crisis, have been ruled incompatible with divine love.

So John uses the concepts and conceits of the apocalyptic genre he knows we want to hear, but he uses them to weave a very different story, one filled with prophetic hope.[15] Revelation is the apocalypse that turns our apocalyptic fantasies upside down—a Trojan horse.

John knows his audience wants revenge. He understands their desire for a tale of retribution, a cathartic release for all their frustration over how unfair the world is. So he studies the genre, uses the tropes, and employs the imagery, all in service of turning those vengeful fantasies upside down. At every twist, John will present us with the apocalypse we think we want, only to pull back the curtain to show us who God really is. He will use the despair of apocalypse to tell us we need something more than revenge.[16] We need hope.

3

THE UNDERGROUND PROPHETIC

If Revelation isn't an apocalypse (at least in the sense we expect), what is it? Well, the short answer is that Revelation is a prophecy. That might not seem groundbreaking; people have been treating Revelation like a road map for the end of time for years. And isn't that exactly what a prophecy is all about? In a word, no. At least not as prophecy comes to us from the Hebrew Scriptures. Hebrew prophecy is absolutely not about predicting the future. It may offer a take on future events or provide an image for what may come, but for the most part, those future events are presented as possibilities.

This is one of the critical differences between apocalypse and prophecy as genres. Prophecy is inherently hopeful. That's not to say that prophecy is happy or perhaps even optimistic; the prophets were often a pretty gloomy group. Still, prophecy, in contrast to apocalypse, leaves open the possibility for change.

You've probably come across the idea that prophecy is not fortune-telling; it is truth-telling. This is true—undoubtedly—and a rich frame for what prophecy is aimed at. But we also have to understand that the whole point of this truth-telling is to effect change. The Hebrew prophets repeatedly challenge authority by saying, "What you are doing is wrong, and if you don't turn from your ways, destruction is on the horizon."

In a sense, this speaks to the future. It predicts what could happen. But the prophetic tradition is pointing to the future specifically to change the present. Ironically, then, prophetic voices assume that the future is not yet written, and that repentance can alter the course of our lives. The prophetic tradition refuses to maintain a hard distinction between the righteous and the wicked, because prophecy maintains that evil is a function of our choices and trusts that the act of truth-telling can awaken us to new possibilities.

Think of the story of Jonah here. The prophet doesn't want to go to Nineveh. He doesn't think they will respond to his prophesying anyway. He certainly doesn't want them to experience any form of divine grace if they do. These Assyrians were his enemies and had done terrible things to his people.

And so unsurprisingly, after being pushed and pulled and famously forced by extraordinary means to go to Nineveh, Jonah gives what could be described as the worst performance by a prophet in a leading role ever. He walks to the center of town and says, "Forty more days and Nineveh will be overturned" (see Jonah 3:4). That's it. His whole pitch. His entire sermon. His only attempt to speak the truth.

But what happens? A tsunami of repentance that should clue us in to the fact that the entire book is meant as a farce. A comedic look at the unrelenting grace of God that shows up where we least expect it and transforms hearts we thought were stone. Nineveh is indeed overturned, but certainly not in the way the prophet had hoped. So Jonah proceeds to pout and complain about God's compassion. It's okay to chuckle; it's a comedy, after all. But even here in Jonah we see the hopeful edge that defines the prophetic tradition. Repentance is always possible even where we would never imagine. Change is only a word away. And God never gives up on any of us, even when we wish God would.

PROPHECY ≠ APOCALYPSE

Revelation is an apocalypse in form—it's weird and violent and otherworldly—but it's a prophecy at heart, utterly convinced that the world can be healed. John applies apocalyptic techniques, but he makes them new by infusing the hope of the prophetic.[1] All things will be made new in this story (Revelation 21:5).

So here's where we need to start to talk about structure.

A defining characteristic of Revelation, which has led to many unfortunate interpretations, is that the text is challenging to organize into any type of chronological structure. The story doesn't seem to flow in a straight line. Instead, it loops back on itself—repeatedly. One of the earliest people to notice this was Saint Victorinus (d. ca. 303 CE). He said that images in the book appear to be "synchronous rather than successive."[2] His argument here was that Revelation repeats the same message multiple times using different images. John's point is not that Christ overcomes evil over and over again. Christ overcomes evil on the cross. The end. However, there are many ways to conceptualize and communicate this. John recognizes precisely that the cross is too big to be communicated in one image, so he throws everything he can think of at us, including the metaphorical kitchen sink.

Victorinus may have been the first, but he's certainly not the last to recognize this phenomenon. One of the preeminent scholars of Revelation, Elisabeth Schüssler Fiorenza, writes that Revelation is "not chronologically ordered but theologi-cally-thematically conceived."[3] That's an elegant way of think-ing about Revelation because it opens up multiple avenues to make sense of the images we're reading. John never imagined us building a complex timeline with each beast and dragon and battle mapped out in excruciating linear detail. Instead, he hoped we might sit back, immersed in the images, marveling at all the ways we see salvation come alive in Jesus. Revelation is telling us the same story from different vantage points. And each time the story repeats, we add a new perspective to our faith, a new commitment to the way of Jesus, and new confi-dence in the lordship of Christ.

In Revelation, there is personal transformation. That is salvation. There's politics and the crumbling of empires built on violence and greed. That is also salvation. There's the dis-arming of evil and the cosmic triumph of life over death. And that, too, is salvation. But all this is part of one story about how Jesus saves the world. For John, none of these perspec-tives are at odds. Personal transformation, social justice, and cosmic healing are implications of a victory already won. The challenge is expanding our imagination wide enough to take it all in.

None of this is meant to imply that Revelation is just a jumble of images slapped together. There is an artistry that is lost in our attempts to put it all on a timeline. And there is a method in the madness that's important to understand. That method comes from the Jewish prophetic tradition: one story, told three times, with expanding scope, just like the texts of the Hebrew prophets.

Revelation leans on Zechariah, Ezekiel, and Daniel throughout. It borrows from extra-biblical apocalyptic texts mimicking form and style. We'll see all these connections as we make our way deeper into the text. But Revelation borrows its structure from the prophet Isaiah. John recontextualizes Isaiah more than any other prophet[4]—at some points even placing the prophet's words in the mouth of his characters (Isaiah 25:8; Revelation 21:4)—but critically, it's the prophetic vision of Isaiah that gives this book shape.

ROUND ONE

Jan Fekkes's *Isaiah and Prophetic Traditions in the Book of Revelation*[5] lays out much of the dependence I'm arguing for here. Understanding how the text of Isaiah builds expanding cycles of concern and salvation gives us, in a lot of ways, a blueprint for what John is doing in Revelation.

At the foundation of Isaiah is a concern for the people of Israel. The prophet opens, "Your rulers are rebels, partners with thieves; they all love bribes and chase after gifts. They do not defend the cause of the fatherless; the widow's case does not come before them" (Isaiah 1:23). As scholar Joseph Blenkinsopp notes, this opening salvo is "addressed to a plurality, but the description is that of a bruised and battered individual."[6] Yet the ultimate scope of this text is wide—a future where weapons will be turned into tools of food production and even the natural order of the animal kingdom will be tilted toward peace. Big ambitions. But the prophet starts by addressing the individual's lived experience. The powerless are being ignored. The powerful are enriching themselves. Therefore, God is no longer interested in worship. "When you spread out your hands in prayer, I hide my eyes from you; even when you offer many prayers, I am not listening" (1:15).

What does God want instead? God wants us to "learn to do right; seek justice. Defend the oppressed. Take up the cause of the fatherless; plead the case of the widow" (Isaiah 1:17);

then we "'will be called the City of Righteousness, the Faithful City.' Zion will be delivered with justice" (1:26–27). According to the prophet Isaiah, salvation is the call to repentance that illuminates the cost of our individual choices, involves us with restorative justice, and saves us from ruin. In other words, God cares about us as individuals. Both individuals who suffer under the unjust choices of others and those individuals who are called to transformation in the light of God's grace.[7] Remember, the prophetic imagination believes that you and I can change, and Isaiah models that prophetic hope. John will follow his lead.

Revelation opens with seven letters to the seven churches, addressing everyday experiences of injustice and anxiety and Christ's call to live with each other well. This is where salvation begins for John—the healing of our relationships and the right ordering of our actions, just as we see in the prophetic tradition. Whether John addresses internal debate and competing factions, as he does Pergamum, conflict with the surrounding culture, as we see with Smyrna, or lack of concern for those in need, as he calls out in Laodicea, the focus is shaping a life that looks like the way of Jesus. In fact, taken against the whole of Revelation, the striking aspect of this opening, just as we see in Isaiah, is the earthiness of the images and language. These prophets call us to change—to course-correct—because salvation starts small. This, however, is just the beginning of the scope of the prophetic imagination.

ROUND TWO

Next, Isaiah pushes the story out a bit more.

At the start of Isaiah 13, the prophet prepares us for the shift by telling us that we are entering a new vision (13:1); in the same way, at the start of Revelation 4, John tells us he was "in the Spirit" again (see Revelation 1:10; 4:2). Both statements signal "a kind of second beginning."[8] For these visionaries, the story of salvation has started over, this time with the camera pulled back a bit further.

However, we are not starting a new story about a new day of the Lord in Isaiah. We are simply looking at the tale from a new perspective. If God truly is Lord, that understanding can't stop at heart level—it must change our social structures as well. In Isaiah the images shift toward a showdown between God and nations. In Revelation, we see strange creatures (Revelation 4:6–8), deadly riders (6:1–8), and natural disturbances that affect the sun, moon, and stars (8:12). In both scenarios, we are confronted with images that seem to pit the goodness of God against the armies of the world (Isaiah 13:4; cf. Revelation 9:16). But the end is the same for both. The victory of God that has changed our hearts now topples our empires. And this, too, is salvation.

The full text of Isaiah is a compilation of several prophetic writings pulled together across a wide swath of time. Assyria, and then later Babylon, were the dominant powers of the era. They marched through much of ancient Palestine, conquering most of the nations, including the northern and later the southern kingdoms of Israel.

And they—as empires are—were terrible. They took slaves and exiled families. They conquered and crushed nations under their war machines. Still, the same salvation that Isaiah first envisions also trusts that this violence can be undone. Look at this image from a little later in Isaiah: "Listen, a noise on the mountains, like that of a great multitude! Listen, an uproar among the kingdoms, like nations massing together!" (Isaiah 13:4). Here the nations have come to think they are powerful enough to fight against God. This is an Armageddon-like confrontation—probably the very conflict that Revelation's Armageddon is modeled after. However, just when the opposition is amassed, Isaiah says that on that day of the Lord, "all hands will go limp, every heart will melt with fear. Terror will seize them, pain and anguish will grip them; they will writhe like a woman in labor. They will look aghast at each other" (13:7–8). Not much of a battle, really. God wins.

The loss is not all bad for the nations. Isaiah also tells us that when the day of the Lord comes, "they will beat their swords into plowshares and their spears into pruning hooks. Nation will not take up sword against nation, nor will they train for war anymore" (Isaiah 2:4). The key here is that the prophet shifts to using political imagery that serves as a polemic against empire itself. Yes, the day of the Lord is about learning to leave our injustice behind and treat our neighbors fairly, but it is not only that. It is also the end of the systems and structures that prop up and justify our violence against each other in the first place. Salvation is the undoing of war as well.

Isaiah is speaking here to a specific empire—the Babylonian Empire and its destruction at the hands of the Medes[9]—yet in Isaiah's vision, the city of Babylon has become more than just a geographic location. It has become a "symbol of enmity toward God."[10] Babylon is more than a city in Isaiah—it is a rejection of God's peace, and John will very specifically pick this up in his writing. In Revelation, the long-gone city of Babylon will reappear. There the name Babylon will stand in for the city of Rome, but just as in Isaiah, the city is a metaphor for something much bigger. Babylon, Rome, Sin City—the issue is not geography. It is coordinated opposition to the way of God and how all things—even our politics—will be transformed by peace. And so, as both prophets unveil God's activity in the world, they shift from the personal to the political because this too is salvation.

ROUND THREE

We're not done yet. As the scholar Joseph Blenkinsopp says of Isaiah, these images are part of a "larger canvas of a projected cataclysm or singularity, a 'Day of Yahveh,' affecting the entire cosmos."[11] Isaiah expands its scope once again. This time with its sights set on the final defeat of evil.

Israel, Assyria, Babylon, politics, empires, and battles—that is all left behind as the prophet turns our attention to creation itself. Earlier, Isaiah warns that "Death expands its jaws, opening wide its mouth" (Isaiah 5:14) and "the earth will be completely laid waste and totally plundered" (24:3), but now we see that God will "swallow up death forever. The Sovereign LORD will wipe away the tears from all faces" (25:8). This might already sound familiar, because it also happens to be one of the most famous lines from Revelation (Revelation 21:4). However, we should keep in mind that Isaiah is a Hebrew prophetic text, and the Hebrew perspective was not particularly preoccupied with any kind of afterlife. It's easy for those steeped in the Christian story to read about the swallowing up of death and immediately jump to thoughts of heaven. But that's not necessarily what's going on here for Isaiah. He is instead describing a day of the Lord that will transform and bring justice to our personal relationships, that will topple our corrupt structures and systems, and that will one day undo the forces of death and disorder completely.[12] For the prophet Isaiah, the personal becomes political, which becomes cosmic because everything God surveys falls within the scope of salvation. The end of death is not an escape to heaven; rather, it is the transformation of life.

And John, who has been taking his cues from Isaiah all along, stays in lockstep.

At the end of John's second vision, he flat out tells us that the world has become "the kingdom of our Lord and of his Messiah" (Revelation 11:15). Christ is enthroned in our hearts. Christ is enthroned in the world. But when John begins the third telling, he says that the time has come for destroying that which destroys the earth (11:18). This is the cosmic expansion of salvation that Isaiah has already laid the groundwork for.

Notice that John does not say, Now comes the time to destroy the world. That is a terrible misreading of Revelation and one that has somehow found far too much purchase in our popular imaginations. Remember, Revelation is not an apocalypse in the way we expect, and John is not pessimistic about the future at all. John does not look forward to the destruction of the earth any more than Isaiah did. John is reminding us that Christ has already overcome evil, and God is at work saving all of creation.

Unsurprisingly, this final cycle of Revelation follows exactly what Isaiah has already shown us. We move from the salvation of our person to the transformation of our politics to the cosmic defeat of evil itself. The only thing discarded in Revelation is that which destroys.

However, just as in Isaiah, the stakes have gone up, and the imagery scales accordingly. When we start unpacking these cycles, we find some pretty bizarre images in round two. It's where we find the throne room of God. It's where we encounter the riders of the apocalypse. John pulls our political world apart and reassembles it to reveal it. But just as in Isaiah, the volume gets turned up for the third and final round. Scary-looking riders on horses give way to great red dragons. Enormous armies (Revelation 9:16) give way to literal beasts emerging on land and sea. Just as Isaiah scales his images to match his scope, moving from defending the vulnerable to God's battle with the nations to the swallowing up of death itself, John follows the pattern set out for him, transitioning from local communities to the challenge of Rome, to the defeat of the dragon, which is evil personified.

But it's all still one story. One victory. One day of the Lord for Isaiah, and one resurrection of the Christ for John. Because this is an essential feature of the prophetic tradition—the act that saves our soul is also the salvation that sets the world right.

A LITTLE FURTHER

One last thing is essential, lest we think John is slavish in his fandom of Isaiah. John has employed the shape and style of the apocalyptic genre to great effect. He's playing to his crowd. It's equally clear that underneath it all, John is far from your run-of-the-mill apocalyptist. He's deeply shaped by the prophetic tradition of the Hebrew Scriptures, and not only by their commitment to the hope of repentance, but also by the scope and scale of the salvation that follows. John is a prophet very much in the tradition of Isaiah.

However, John also trusts that in Christ he has encountered the final apocalypse of God, the divine ultimately unveiled before humanity. And because he is convinced that God no longer speaks through mediators but is now revealed directly to us in Christ (Hebrews 1:1–2), he is also confident that the final expression of salvation will extend further than Isaiah could have imagined.

If the central call of the book of Isaiah is the hope to trust that God will do something new (Isaiah 43:19), John's intent is to push that even further. Or as he misquotes Isaiah, "Behold, I make all things new" (Revelation 21:5 KJV). That's not a coincidence or a typo. That is John watching Isaiah take the hope of salvation and broaden it from the personal to the political to the created order and now asking himself, What if we're just getting started? John is shaping his narrative after the model of Isaiah to demonstrate the prophetic imagination that fuels the Jesus story, but he is also compelled by that story to enlarge things ever further. Far from limiting himself to a single subversive line, John borrows and expands Isaiah's vision over and over again, even taking one of Isaiah's most iconic images, that of the divine warrior, and turning it completely inside out in a pivotal moment of the Revelation narrative.

This should not surprise us, because John's decision to ground himself in the vision of Isaiah and then go even further is quintessentially Jesus-y.

FULFILLED TODAY

> The Spirit of the Lord is on me,
>   because he has anointed me
>   to proclaim good news to the poor.
> He has sent me to proclaim freedom for the prisoners
>   and recovery of sight for the blind,
> to set the oppressed free,
>   to proclaim the year of the Lord's favor.
> (Luke 4:18–19)

Jesus has returned to his hometown. He enters the synagogue, he is handed a scroll, and he reads this passage from the prophet Isaiah. Then he rolls the scroll up, hands it back to the attendant, and sits down. While everyone is either fascinated or flabbergasted by this display, he says to them, "Today this scripture is fulfilled in your hearing" (4:21). It's quite a moment. Jesus, too, grounds his calling in Isaiah's vision.

What's particularly telling is how Jesus, in a model John will follow, expands Isaiah's hope.

The passage Jesus reads comes from Isaiah 61. That's in the final part of Isaiah. Considering that Isaiah covers such a long section of Israel's history, we generally think Isaiah is a compiled text with either two or three sources. But its final section is by far the most hopeful. Isaiah has shifted his attention toward the final salvation of the cosmos that we highlighted earlier. However, compare what Jesus reads above to what Isaiah writes below.

> The Spirit of the Sovereign LORD is on me,
>   because the LORD has anointed me
>   to proclaim good news to the poor.
> He has sent me to bind up the brokenhearted,
>   to proclaim freedom for the captives
>   and release from darkness for the prisoners,
> to proclaim the year of the LORD's favor
>   and the day of vengeance of our God.
> (Isaiah 61:1–2a)

Right away, we've got an exciting anomaly because when Jesus reads from the prophet, he says he has come to proclaim the year of the Lord's favor. And then he stops.

Isaiah says that the year of the Lord's favor comes tied to the day of God's vengeance. Jesus says, Not exactly. And at this point, we shouldn't be too surprised by Jesus reinterpreting the Hebrew Scriptures for us. One of his favorite things was to take an ancient passage and say, You have heard it said, but now I offer you something new (see Matthew 5:21, 27, 33, 38, 43). However, at the same time, in the same section, in fact, Jesus also tells us that not one jot will disappear from the law until everything is accomplished (Matthew 5:18). Yet here he is in Luke, leaving out at least a few key words. Note the language that Jesus uses as he closes the scroll. He says to his audience, "Today this scripture is fulfilled in your hearing." It's the same language from earlier in Matthew: I have come not to destroy but to fulfill the law (Matthew 5:17). Same word.

That word, *pleroo*, has some range to it, but essentially it means "to bring to completion that which was already begun."[13] And here we have one of the central puzzles of Christian theology. Does bringing the story to its completion mean that every word and every moment carries equal weight in the end—like normalizing audio to make sure every note has a similar volume—or is it better to think of fulfillment in terms of understanding where the story was always headed?

I contend it's the latter. Jesus is saying that when we follow the trajectory of the biblical story, yes, we see that there has been violence throughout human history. Yes, there's been a lot of pain to bear. Yes, there has even been vengeance attributed to God along the way. But ultimately, that's not how the story ends. To fulfill the story, to properly finish the narrative and complete what God started when God breathed life into humanity, is to trust in the day when the Lord's favor conquers unconditionally. Jesus says, Isaiah's vision is where I ground my purpose, but we will have to push even further into hope to complete the story.

Isaiah imagines a day when God would save the world and destroy the evil among us. Jesus transforms that vision into a day when God would save the world by destroying the evil in us.

People sometimes speculate that Jesus separates the day of the Lord's favor here in Luke from the day of the Lord's vengeance upon his return, imagining an outpouring of Jesus-endorsed violence at some point in the distant future. But that, too, is a misreading, one that Revelation will make abundantly clear when Jesus finally arrives to undermine those vengeful fantasies for good.

What Jesus introduces here and brings to completion on the cross is the mysterious apocalypse of God's wrath against the godlessness and wickedness that harms us (Romans 1:18). Jesus reveals that all will be conquered by love on the day of the Lord, but the surprise is that God's vengeance was only ever intended for all that damages God's creation. And the day of the Lord's favor on us is when God makes all things new by destroying the anti-God powers of Sin and Death.[14]

That the prophets couldn't quite get there does nothing to diminish their contributions. They transformed our relationship to the divine, orienting us toward a just world as the fruit of our repentance. Jesus now extends the story by revealing that even our most hopeful expectations fall short of God's grace.

Time and time again in Revelation, our anger and frustration will be shown to us, and then overturned by the power of transformative grace. Our tendency toward apocalyptic pessimism will be offered up and then upended. Even our most hopeful imaginations of the divine, those profound images gathered and preserved by the prophets, will find themselves turned upside down and handed back more beautiful than when they began. Nothing is left untouched by Jesus.

4

STARTING LOCAL

I know we're excited to get to the good stuff, all those beasts and riddles and apocalyptic fodder. However, it's essential that we ground ourselves first in the seven letters to the seven churches. After all, Revelation is structured using Isaiah as a template. And Isaiah is convinced that our encounters with God transform our lived experience of community. Only that awakening can challenge our politics and upend evil's grip on creation. That story, in three stages, is crucial to John's vision.

And this has always been intriguing about Revelation—for a book that ends with the transformation of all things, it begins modestly with some advice for local churches. Still, this opening cycle follows the same pattern as the next two. John is taken into the Spirit for a vision (Revelation 1:10), which ends with Jesus enthroned in the world (3:21). Even though it's tempting to jump straight to the wacky stuff, it's essential to move at a measured pace, understanding that John, taking cues from Isaiah, knows that the renewal of all things begins with the transformation of our hearts.

In Christianity, the classical approach after we talk about salvation is to talk about sanctification—all the good stuff that happens in us as we grow and change to become more like

Christ. One of the shortcomings of traditional formulations of sanctification is that they can become too inward-focused; a sanctification of the soul that fails to leave any footprints in the world. Think of Christians who obsessively fret over impure thoughts but somehow fail to allow their trust in Jesus to influence choices at the voting booth or online checkout. Far too often, our imagination of what it means to be sanctified stays in our heads.

Revelation means to disabuse us of that notion by connecting our personal story to the healing of the world. And that's precisely why a book that wants to turn our imagination of everything upside down starts with how Jesus turns small fledgling communities right side up. After all, Jesus says that the kingdom of God is like a mustard seed—slow, steady growth will change the world.

PERSECUTION FANTASIES

The seven letters are an engrossing mix of agendas. They address conflict with neighbors, accommodation to cultural exceptions, and even complacency in the Christian community, but they do this by straddling a line between managing specific moments in particular places and speaking to a larger, more diverse audience—namely us. There were particular human beings who received these letters. At the same time, John reiterates that the message is for all who have an ear to hear what the Spirit says (Revelation 2:7, 11, 17, 29; 3:6, 13, 22). We have to keep that tension in mind, because while the message is for us, it depends on the unique circumstances of these communities.

For example, some of the people reading Revelation were acutely aware of the pressures on them. To the church in Ephesus, John writes, "You have persevered and have endured hardships for my name, and have not grown weary" (2:3). In other words, good job.

Other communities were in entirely different situations. Persecution may have only been on the horizon. To the church in Smyrna, John writes, "Do not be afraid of what you are about to suffer" (2:10). That's an ominous greeting.

Later, he writes to the church in Laodicea to say, "You say, 'I am rich; I have acquired wealth and do not need a thing.' But you do not realize that you are wretched, pitiful, poor, blind and naked" (3:17). Clearly, not every church community had the same experience of the Roman Empire.

And this actually lines up with our best understanding of the period under Domitian. Persecution, if we can call it that, was "local and sporadic," ranging from "verbal harassment" to accusations "prompting officials to investigate" Christian communities.[1] Domitian was much more interested in going after his political rivals than becoming preoccupied with a new cult out in the country.

This is important, though, because it shows us that John had a realistic grasp of what these communities were facing.[2] It means he knew these people and had likely traveled to spend time with these communities, and rather than fan the flames of conspiratorial thinking, working to build up and then capitalize on their fears, he speaks plainly and honestly about the truth of their situation. For an apocalypse, Revelation opens with a fairly level-headed threat assessment. It's a good reminder that we do not need to conjure up fantasies of persecution to identify with what we read here.

That's not to say that apocalyptic imagery isn't present in the letters. The very fact that John chooses seven churches, a number he will come back to for seven seals, and seven trumpets, and seven bowls, should tell us that these communities are chosen as part of the larger spiraling narrative arc that shapes Revelation. These communities are unique, but they are also chosen as representative of the range of Christian experience.

FAST FACTS FROM THE SEVEN LETTERS

For the scope of this book, we're not going to try to look deeply into each of the seven letters. We don't have the space to do justice to that project. However, here are a few facts that might spark your imagination as you read through the seven letters on your own.

In Ephesus, one of the main attractions was the temple of Artemis. This temple featured an asylum tree at its center. Any criminal who made their way to that tree was free from capture.[3] The faithful community in that city is promised the opportunity to eat from the tree of life in a fun little nod to local geography (Revelation 2:7). God's grace is like their tree, scaled up.

In Sardis, John does something similar. Roughly five hundred years before he writes, the acropolis in Sardis was captured when a soldier climbed the mountain face and snuck into the city.[4] And then, some two centuries later, it happened again.[5] Records from the time blame the defensive fault on a lack of vigilance.[6] So when John yells at the church, "Wake up!," he's likely playing off that local history.

Finally, to the (ancient) city of brotherly love, Philadelphia, John offers these words: "What he opens no one can shut, and what he shuts no one can open" (3:7). Unsurprisingly, this is a reference to the prophet Isaiah. There, the servant Eliakim is elevated to an important role under the king and given a key to the house of David (Isaiah 22:22). What's important is that the key being handed over isn't the key to the city gates; this is not the authority to let people in or keep them out. This is the key to the grain storehouses. In other words, Eliakim is given the responsibility to look after the people by deciding when to open the resources to those in need and when to save for future concerns. For the community in Philadelphia, this reference is John's encouragement to live up to their name, to use what resources the community had to care for neighbors in need. If God has opened doors to us, we should not close ours to others.

It is intriguing how local all these examples are. John is searching for ways to begin with the particular before moving to the universal. And this, I think, is important. For a book that wants to direct our attention to the way that Jesus has overthrown death and Hades, it understands that salvation begins when we pay attention to the needs of our neighbors. A disembodied salvation from evil that does not address poverty and racism or the specific contours of our neighborhood is untenable for John. In this way we see again the influence of the embodied Jesus of the Gospels—the one who felt the hunger of his audience in his gut and fed them (Mark 6:31–44).

In fact, this opening salvo from John reminds me of the brother of Jesus, James. Perhaps John might paraphrase his thoughts this way, "If Jesus has conquered death, and defeated evil, and overcome Caesar but does not address our physical needs, what good is that victory?" (cf. James 2:16). James's concern for the poor is very possibly born from his lived experience. The earliest Gospel narratives that address Jesus' home-life show a devoted father in Joseph, but he is conspicuously absent later in Jesus' life. We don't know what happened to Joseph but as a younger brother to Jesus, James, growing up in a single-parent home and exposed to too many social pressures, developed a theology with a heart for the vulnerable. It seems that John, in the same way, has channeled his lived experience of the Roman Empire into tangible expressions of judicial reform, awareness of vulnerability, and social responsibility. This is not the pessimism we expect from an apocalypse—the "trash it all, let God sort it out" mentality. This opening salvo affirms Revelation's commitment to transformation.

Still, there is one more image in the address to Laodicea that will bring us back to the activist stream that runs through the book.

LUKEWARM WATERS

For some, this is probably the one you've been waiting for. Lukewarm water spit out of God's mouth is a provocative image, after all (Revelation 3:16). I get it. We've probably all heard those awkward sermons about how God would rather you go hog wild in sin than sit stone-cold in church. That, of course, feels inherently odd. And your instincts are right. It is a flawed interpretation of this image.

Laodicea was a city that had three main economic drivers. A medical school specializing in ophthalmology drew in students and dollars from a large region of the empire. A banking sector that benefited from travel through the city kept the money flowing through town. And there was a unique and booming wool export industry built around a particular type of black sheep that locals had cultivated.[7] When we hear the counsel to buy gold from God (rather than trust your banks) so you can wear white clothes (rather than fine black wool) and receive salve to soothe your eyes (rather than the Phrygian powder used in the ophthalmology school), this is a very particular set of challenges uniquely tailored to the community in Laodicea.[8] Banking and black clothing and medical care are not problematic in themselves. What can be a problem is the way our participation in the status quo can put the squeeze on others.

Laodicea was doing well. They were wealthy and comfortable, and this is essential for us to hear. Revelation is not a book written exclusively to the oppressed; it is also a book written explicitly for those who benefit laterally from oppression. John wants us to see the underside of the empire, the way it feeds off the vulnerable. And comfort makes those realities hard to see. To bring that to the surface, John once again uses a local reference.

Laodicea had a strong economy. What they didn't have was fresh water. The river Lycus that fed the city would often dry up, leaving Laodicea to import water. Luckily, there were two fantastic sources nearby, and the resources to access them.

First, there were hot springs to the north in Hierapolis. I live near the Rocky Mountains, and this type of mineral-laden hot springs is a huge tourist draw. In the ancient world, they were also prized for their ability to clean and heal wounds. Aqueducts from Hierapolis down to Laodicea were constructed in the first century and remain visible today.[9] The problem was, these hot springs would have cooled considerably after the five-mile tumble to Laodicea. And because of the minerals, the water was helpful for all kinds of needs but, unfortunately, not drinking.

Luckily, Colossae was close by to the south. Colossae had a fantastic, reliable source of meltwater that came off Mount Cadmus.[10] We probably don't think of snowy mountains in Jesus' world, but Laodicea sits at roughly the same latitude as Colorado. Elevation matters. Colossae was damaged badly by an earthquake in 61 CE, well before the time of Revelation, but water continued to flow down the mountain through the ruins, reaching Laodicea some eleven miles away. But after its flow through Turkish heat, the water that reached Laodicea was decidedly lukewarm. Perfectly drinkable but not nearly as refreshing as when it had started its journey.

In this image is a wealthy community of people who think they need nothing yet are entirely dependent on mineral water from their neighbors to the north and clean water from their friends to the south. John's point is that the self-sufficiency of Laodicea is an illusion. Wealth can make us think we deserve what flows to us. You can be healing waters for those who are wounded, or you can be cold, refreshing streams for those who thirst; just don't settle into the kind of wealth that collects passively without intentionally giving back. Because that's revolting, and the measure of our faith is not how well we are doing; it is how well we serve those near us.

THE NARROW VICTORY

> To the one who is victorious, I will give the right to sit with me on my throne, just as I was victorious and sat down with my Father on his throne. Whoever has ears, let them hear what the Spirit says to the churches. (Revelation 3:21–22)

And so we reach the end of the letters and the end of the first round of the story of Revelation. Christ is victorious and has sat with God to rule the world—there are two more cycles to come as the revelation expands up and out—but for now, Christ reigns. And this is key to understanding what will come in the apocalypse. John sees no option but for Christ's self-sacrifice to change the world. The cross influences our relationship to our neighbor, it transforms our participation in the politic around us, it inspires more to follow the way of Jesus that will inevitably heal the cosmos.

But that way is embodied in specific communities and circumstances, which is why a story that ends with the destruction of evil has to start in localized expressions of good. Any reading of Revelation that doesn't inspire us to the neighbor love that crosses our imaginary boundaries and welcomes back those we have pushed away has missed the revealed Jesus.

In Matthew's gospel, Jesus is wrapping up his first major public address when he says, "Enter through the narrow gate. For wide is the gate and broad is the road that leads to destruction, and many enter through it. But small is the gate and narrow the road that leads to life, and only a few find it" (Matthew 7:13–14). When we hear language like this—whether from Jesus or in the Apocalypse—we often imagine that God has finally had enough of us. Turn or burn and all that. But that's not really what's going on here. God is always for us, always on our side. And all that God has made will be healed in the end. After all, even those who are spiritually bankrupt will be offered a place in the upside-down kingdom (Matthew 5:3). Still, these words, *destruction* and *narrow*, scare us. Often, I think, because we would rather assign them to God than acknowledge our complicity. Except, the word Jesus uses here is *apóleia*. In Greek, this refers to rubble or ruin, spoilage or waste, a pile of destruction, if you prefer. This is where Jesus says the wide road, the default path leads. There is no destroyer in Jesus' warning, no threat to end us if we choose poorly. There is only the path we choose and where it takes us. That is very much the story of Revelation.

The conventional way in the world, the one that prizes wealth and security and comfort and pleasure, even if it comes at the cost of our neighbor, will slowly crumble in on itself.

But there is an exit ramp if only we can open our eyes to see it. The way of self-giving and neighbor love, the way of proactive justice that seeks out what is wrong below the surface to ensure that all are cared for. A road that is narrow not because it's hard, but because it's hidden, off to the side of our view, a way we have to search for. This is the beauty of the

Scriptures; they hint at an alternative route in the world. One that eschews religious violence and welcomes foreigners and widows. One that starts small and grows uncontrollably. One that turns everything upside down and implicates us in the sanctification of the cosmos.

As theologian Dorothee Sölle writes, "The message of Jesus is that the more you grow in love, the more vulnerable you make yourself. You have fewer securities and weapons."[11] Revelation will turn its attention to our weapons and violence soon, but before that we are asked to consider our securities. Where do we place our trust and how vulnerable are we willing to be in the immediate communities that surround us? Peace in one leads to peace expanded. That's the narrow path that heals the world. For John, the transformation of the cosmos begins in faithful, local communities that care for each other.

5

THE (SOME) ONE ON
THE THRONE

In the opening chapters of Revelation, John recounts the story of Christ's victory through the lens of community. This first telling of that story is at the level of our personal transformation and the way it shapes our local activism. From an apocalyptic standpoint, things have been pretty tame so far. While there have been some provocative images, the opening could reasonably sit alongside the epistles of the New Testament.

Still, the first cycle of Revelation opens with John's declaration that he was "in the Spirit" (Revelation 1:10), and it ends with the exclamation that Christ is victorious and sitting with the Father on his throne (3:21). This is the signal that we are about to begin again.

The second cycle begins the same way with a vision (4:2). And it concludes with the same victory as God begins to reign on the earth (11:17). We are about to read the story again.[1]

However, since we are moving from the realm of our personal transformation to the arena of our politics, this time the story will be told with imagery designed to encourage us to think a little bigger. The stakes will get higher, the images more subversive.

THE FOUR LIVING CREATURES

> At once I was in the Spirit, and there before me was a
> throne in heaven with someone sitting on it. And the one
> who sat there had the appearance of jasper and ruby. A
> rainbow that shone like an emerald encircled the throne.
> Surrounding the throne were twenty-four other thrones,
> and seated on them were twenty-four elders. They were
> dressed in white and had crowns of gold on their heads.
> From the throne came flashes of lightning, rumblings and
> peals of thunder. (Revelation 4:2–5)

There are also four living creatures—covered with eyes,
each having six wings. One has the face of a lion, the second has the face of an ox, the third has a man's face, and the
final one has the face of an eagle. If you were waiting for the
more out-there imagery to appear, we're here. These creatures
come praising this "someone" who sits on the throne. Then
the twenty-four elders also praise the one on the throne. They
even lay their crowns before him, and they say, "You are worthy, our Lord and God, to receive glory and honor and power,
for you created all things, and by your will they were created
and have their being" (4:11).

So we have thrones, crowns, elders, and bizarre living creatures with wings and eyes all over. Despite the absurd descriptions, it's almost easy for us to assume we understand what's
happening here. This is an upside-down apocalypse, though,
so let's take a closer look at these characters. We'll start with
the four living creatures because this image set is relatively easy
to find a precedent for. They come from the book of Ezekiel.

In the Hebrew culture, the images in Ezekiel were consid-
ered so powerful that rumors swirled about the rabbis forbid-
ding anyone under thirty from reading the opening chapters.[2]
In the first chapter, Ezekiel sees a "windstorm coming out of

the north—an immense cloud with flashing lightning and sur-rounded by brilliant light" (1:4; recall the flashes of lightning, rumblings and peals of thunder from John's vision), and in Ezekiel's fire there was what looked like four living creatures. "In appearance, their form was human, but each of them had four faces and four wings" (1:5–6). Ezekiel writes that "each of the four had the face of a human being, and on the right side each had the face of a lion, and on the left the face of an ox; each also had the face of an eagle" (1:10).

In John's vision, each creature has one face; in Ezekiel's, they each have four faces, but it's pretty clear that John is drawing from familiar Hebrew imagery here. And that was common.

A nonbiblical text called the *Apocalypse of Abraham* was probably written between 75 and 150 CE—about the same time that John was writing Revelation. The writer says, "I saw under the fire a throne and round about it the watchfulness of many eyes. Under the throne, four fiery living ones singing, and each had four faces. Each had the face of a lion, a man, an ox and an eagle, and because of their four heads upon their bodies they each had sixteen faces. Each one also had three pairs of wings."[3]

The bottom line is that this image of creatures with mul-tiple faces, lots of eyes, and wings all over was a common one in Hebrew literature. At a basic level, what is going on is quite simple. This is an image of a rightly ordered universe. The images of a wild animal, a domestic animal, a bird, and a human face make up the picture of the entire world sur-rounding God and giving praise.[4] What's with all the eyes? Well, in ancient Near Eastern literature, eyes and the language of watchfulness represented wisdom or vision of what was right and true.[5] Combined together, these creatures represent a creation wise enough, seeing clearly enough, to worship well.

Interestingly, Christian theologians would later come along and take these images of lion, ox, human, and eagle and ascribe them to the Gospels. Saint Victorinus of Petrovium in the third century pointed this out—that God has given us four different images of Jesus that correspond to the different images in Revelation, and together, they give us a rightly ordered picture of the Christ.

THE TWENTY-FOUR ELDERS AND THE ROMAN COURT

While the four living creatures come from the world of Hebrew prophecy, there is no direct parallel in Jewish literature for the twenty-four elders. There were twenty-four groups of priests and musicians in 1 Chronicles 24:7–19; 25:1–31, and some have suggested that since both groups are involved in worship maybe this is the inspiration for John's image.[6] There are also twenty-four gates and features named for the twelve tribes and the twelve apostles in the city of the new Jerusalem (Revelation 21:12–14). That's definitely an interesting connection, and one John may be keeping in his back pocket for later. Still, John calls these figures elders. The term is *presbuteroi*, which was used for overseers in the early Christian communities, but it's not a common term in Hebrew texts. This image seems to be drawn from somewhere else.

Surprisingly, this is not a biblical image; it's a Roman one.

Just before the time of Jesus and well before the time of John, there was instability within the Roman Empire. Julius Caesar went to war with the Senate, eventually establishing his control over Rome. A few years later, he was assassinated, which threw the empire into a long season of chaos as people fought for control. Eventually, Julius's grand-nephew Octavian defeated his rivals and declared himself Caesar Augustus.

He was heralded as the one who saved Rome by quelling the civil war and bringing peace to the world.

Augustus was a shrewd politician who played off his popularity to develop what we now call the emperor cult. He led the Roman Senate to grant the title *Divus Iulius* (the divine Julius) to his predecessor in January 42 BCE. He even pointed to the appearance of a comet in July of 44 BCE as proof of Julius's divinity, taking the title *Divi filius* (Son of the divine) for himself. Through this, he established that his "father," Julius Caesar (actually his great-uncle), had fulfilled his purpose on earth in establishing the role of emperor and had now taken his place among the Roman pantheon as a god.

This, of course, made Augustus a son of a god, which is how the imperial cult came to work. The dead emperor was deified, and the new emperor was worshiped on earth as the protector of the peace, the son of a god—the one to whom all knees should bow in service.

For Augustus, the emperor was not a god himself but as close as one could possibly be. This meant that a whole new economy developed in the Roman Empire as important cities wanting to increase their trade relationships with Rome built new stadiums and agoras and temples dedicated to the godlike emperor in power. These displays of fealty often culminated in the gift of golden crowns. Josephus records gifts of crowns given in recognition of Roman conquerors Pompey and Titus,[7] and Tacitus records that a vassal king would remove his crown and place it on the statue of the emperor in a symbol of subordination.[8] By the time of Vespasian, it was standard practice for city leaders to do this, and when he was acclaimed emperor in the year 69 CE, he was given golden crowns from all the cities across the empire, inscribed with "Our savior and benefactor, the only worthy emperor of Rome, Vespasian."[9]

However, during all this time, the emperor remained a man, not a god on earth. In fact, Vespasian had taken steps to move the empire back toward a republic, giving power back to the Senate and working to make Rome more like a democracy. When he died, his son Titus took control and continued in that direction as well. Titus even refused to take the title of emperor. But when he died only two years later, his brother Domitian took over and changed everything.

DOMITIAN AND THE IMPERIAL COURT

Domitian was very different. He had been sidelined to secondary roles during the reigns of both his father and brother. When he was made emperor, he began setting to right what he saw as a grave injustice.[10] He began to purge those loyal to his father's intentions,[11] systematically dismantling the democratic work his father had done, moving the center of government exclusively to the imperial court and making the Senate almost purely ceremonial. He saw Rome as a divine monarchy with himself at the head. According to the Roman historian Suetonius, Domitian even gave himself the title *Dominus et Deus*—"lord and god"—and required everyone to address him this way.[12] Now, it's worth noting that the veracity of Suetonius's claims about Domitian have been brought into question by some historians who think he may have indulged in some hyperbole. But the presence of his writing indicates that, at the very least, there was a popular imagination of Domitian as unreasonably egotistical.[13] For example, Domitian had twenty-four *lictores* that attended to him.[14] A *lictor* was a court employee that was part servant and part bodyguard, and Domitian demanded twice the typical number assigned to an emperor.[15] He also hired an imperial choir to follow him in public singing his praises while wearing imperial wreaths similar to the description in Revelation.[16]

Domitian set out ambitious plans to recapture the glory of Rome under Augustus: new wars to expand the borders,[17] massive construction projects across the empire, and reviving the emperor cult with renewed vigor—this time, however, with the emperor as a living deity in Rome.[18]

As such, Domitian took great pains to align his reign with Jupiter, the head of the Roman pantheon. He first built a chapel to Jupiter and then enlarged it into an enormous temple after his coronation.[19] Next, Domitian set up his own games to honor Jupiter. The Capitoline Games included gladiatorial combat and poetry competitions and were designed to reinforce Domitian's deity. When he appeared at the games, he was flanked by the high priest of Jupiter on one side and the high priest of the imperial cult on the other, each wearing a crown bearing his name. This made Domitian the center of religious fervor. The crowds in attendance were required to wear white and joined the court choir as they sang praises: "Hail, Victory, Lord of the earth, Invincible, Power, Glory, Honor, Peace, Security, Holy, Blessed, Great, Unequalled, Though Alone, Worthy art Thou, Worthy is he to inherit the Kingdom, Come, come, do no delay, Come again."[20]

In fact, a gold coin of Domitian was commissioned that depicted the thunderbolts of Jupiter above his throne,[21] reminiscent of John's image of the lightning and peals of thunder that he witnesses coming from the throne (Revelation 4:5). John further describes the image of the one upon the throne appearing as jasper and carnelian or ruby (4:3). These are all red precious stones that bring to mind the image of *taurobolium*.[22] This practice of sacrificing a bull on a raised platform with the blood pouring down over the one being honored was graphically put to film for the HBO show *Rome*. We don't know whether Domitian ever participated in this practice, but it's likely that the description of robes washed white in blood (7:13–14) is used in subversion of this pagan practice.[23] The image of one on the throne, glistening like a red stone, may also point us back to the emperor again.

However, perhaps most relevant to this comparison is the deification of Domitian's son, who was born to the Empress Domitia in 73 CE and died ten years later. Domitian issued a gold coin in 83 CE embossed with the image of his son sitting atop heaven playing with the seven celestial bodies. At the time, Roman astrologers knew of the sun, moon, Mercury, Venus, Mars, Saturn, and Jupiter. Ancient telescopes could only reach so far. But this was an image of Domitian's son having conquered the universe in death. The inscription on the coin read "The divine Caesar, son of the Emperor Domitian."[24]

Despite all this attention, a particular fascination drove Domitian: the sense that he controlled the destiny of the world. It was widespread practice for an emperor to grant a significant city the privilege of building him a special temple. Several temples might be built across the empire, but the emperor could choose for himself a *neokoros*—a single site to be the center of his worship outside of Rome. The officially endorsed temple, for lack of a better comparison.

Domitian's neokoros was in Ephesus. That's the same Ephesus from Paul's letter to the Ephesians and the same city named in Revelation 2. Ephesus was a major seaport, a thriving trade center. Before Domitian, it was primarily known for its temple to the goddess Artemis. Domitian, however, built his temple right on the water facing the seaport, featuring the largest statue of any of the Caesars that has ever been uncovered. Parts of the figure—the face and right hand—are today housed in the Ephesus Archaeological Museum in Selçuk, Turkey. Estimates put the scale of the entire original statue at well over twenty-seven feet tall. This statue would have been a focal point for the entire city, seated at the entry point into the gate on the site of what is known today as the Temple of Sebastoi. Of particular interest is the gigantic right hand of Domitian, which is curled as if gripping something that has long since been lost. However, another statue of Domitian, this one on display at the Vatican Museums in Vatican City, shows that Domitian was often depicted holding a scroll in his right hand. It's likely that this is what the massive right hand of the statue in Ephesus once held.

THE SIGNIFICANCE OF THE SCROLL

A scroll was an important image in Rome, uniquely important to the Caesars. It symbolized everything that would happen during their lifetime and reign. A scroll in a Caesar's right hand reminds us that the emperor alone controls history, and Domitian, through his visage across the empire, demonstrated that his will and power kept the world together.

You can imagine that this small community of Jesus followers, who believed that the king of the universe came not in strength, power, or displays of grandeur, but in humility, peace, and suffering—to the point that they refused to even acknowledge any Lord but Jesus—became an irritant in the narrative of Domitian. Particularly, perhaps, in his neokoros, Ephesus.

However, it is unlikely that Domitian unleashed systematic persecution and executions of Christians across the empire. We don't have any historical evidence for that. And we know some Christians were doing just fine under the reign of Domitian. Still, for those who refused to worship him, the consequences were likely severe. Domitian would not have tolerated that kind of disrespect. The historian Ethelbert Stauffer writes, "Domitian was the first emperor to recognize that behind the Christian movement there stood an enigmatic figure who threatened the glory of the emperors."[25]

Here's the scenario John has built for us so far in Revelation 4: we have a "someone," whom we are clearly meant to infer is God, sitting on a throne at the center of this opening scene. Around that throne are four living creatures, covered with wings and eyes and faces, an image from the Hebrew Scriptures representing all creation. Traditionally, these creatures sit worshiping God, representing a rightly ordered universe. This is how we might expect a Hebrew prophet to imagine the climax of history.

But next we have twenty-four elders bringing crowns of gold as gifts, an image drawn from the emperor's worship. In particular, the imperial court of Domitian with his twenty-four attendants. This person is powerful; flashes of lightning and rumblings and peals of thunder come from his throne like Jupiter, almost threatening anyone watching. His ruby appearance reminds us of violent pagan rituals. Then, as the attendants take their crowns and present them to the one on the throne, the scene becomes stranger still. They call out to the one on the throne and say, "You are worthy, our Lord and God [*Dominus et Deus*], to receive glory and honor and power, for you created all things, and by your will they were created" (4:11). It sounds beautiful on its own and undoubtedly reminiscent of scriptural worship, but also eerily similar to the acclamation of the emperor.

Why is John pulling together imagery from Hebrew and Roman worship so tightly? Is he acknowledging a syncretism between Rome and Jesus, confessing that our religious ideals often imitate the power of our politics in the end? I'm sure many carried the hope that God might one day show up like an emperor and impose divine justice on the world. That was the apocalyptic hope of the day, after all. Jesus himself spoke at great length about a coming kingdom of heaven. The term *kingdom* absolutely connotes Rome's power and strength, the military and violence. And for a lot of people, that combination probably worked. They wanted their God to be as ruthless as Domitian.

If we find ourselves cheering right now, John has us precisely where he wants us.

REVELATION 5, UNPACKED

> Then I saw in the right hand of him who sat on the throne a scroll with writing on both sides and sealed with seven seals. And I saw a mighty angel proclaiming in a loud voice, "Who is worthy to break the seals and open the scroll?" But no one in heaven or on earth or under the earth could open the scroll or even look inside it. I wept and wept because no one was found who was worthy to open the scroll or look inside. Then one of the elders said to me, "Do not weep! See, the Lion of the tribe of Judah, the Root of David, has triumphed. He is able to open the scroll and its seven seals." (Revelation 5:1–5)

In the movie *The Prestige*, a film about dueling magicians, one of the characters explains that every great magic trick has three parts: The pledge, where the magician shows you something you expect. The turn, where the magician does something unexpected, like make the rabbit disappear. And finally, the prestige, where everything comes full circle and the rabbit comes back. It's not just the magic trick that makes the moment; it's the entire movement through the story that draws you in and leaves you breathless.

I don't know if John liked magic, but I know he loved showmanship.

In this scene, we start with the story of a prophet recounting a vision. John is in the Spirit, and there before him is God. Next, the images slowly contort, and Hebrew worship mingles with Roman imagery. The hope of salvation is tainted with the expectation of vengeance. It takes on a decidedly apocalyptic tone. But now something is wrong.

No one can open the scroll. No one can finish the story. The son has died and ascended to heaven, so the court mourns their loss because no one is worthy to guide the flow of history.

Then John hears about a lion. A mighty conqueror, perhaps someone who can succeed the one who sits on the throne. A worthy heir, one who can muster the ruthlessness it takes to rule the world and direct history the way Domitian has. But when John turns, that is not at all what he sees. What he has been led to expect was an imperial fantasy, but there stands a Lamb, looking as if it had been slain (5:6).

This moment is pulled off with incredible dexterity. We have been set up to expect a savior in the mold of Domitian. The lion is the quintessential symbol of a warrior's strength. Appeals to the "tribe of Judah" and the "Root of David" prime us to imagine redemption in the model of the most successful military king in Israel's history. But all of it is misdirection.

The warrior titles ascribed to the Lamb, the images of the Roman imperial cult, even the conventional images of Hebrew worship, are used as bait to draw us in so our imagination can be wrenched in a new direction by the ultimate image of victory through sacrifice.

There is so much going on here. Jesus is the apocalyptic hope of enemy destruction turned upside down.[26] Jesus is the cult of Domitian and power turned inside out.[27] As the scholar David Barr says, "A more complete reversal of value would be hard to imagine."[28] Even what we might assume to be religious language again defies our expectations. John talks about a Lamb looking as if it had been "slain." However, the Greek word he chooses here is the word *sphazô*, which means something more like slaughtered, or murdered,[29] rather than *thyô*, the word that would generally be associated with ritual sacrifice.[30] In fact, *thyô* appears precisely zero times in Revelation, as John opts for criminal instead of temple metaphors to describe what has happened to Jesus.[31] Jesus is not a religious sacrifice. He is a political victim.

The appearance of the Lamb, who takes the place of everything we have been led to expect, turns all of it, including our religious expectations, upside down. God is not a tyrant like Domitian. God does not rule with threat and intimidation. God does not conquer by demanding ritual violence. The Lamb that was slain was murdered through human violence that reveals the truth of God's nonviolent character to us.

> And they sang a new song, saying:
>   "You are worthy to take the scroll
>   and to open its seals,
>   because you were slain,
>   and with your blood you purchased for God
>   persons from every tribe and language and people
>   and nation
>   You have made them to be a kingdom and priests to
> serve our God,
>   and they will reign on the earth."
> (Revelation 5:9–10)

And we should have seen it coming.

WHO IS ON THE THRONE?

In Jesus' first public address, he opens with the line "Blessed are the poor in spirit, for theirs is the kingdom of heaven" (Matthew 5:3). We're pretty used to the idea of Jesus and his kingdom, and sometimes that hides how provocative this language was.

First of all, "kingdom" is inherently patriarchal language. It presupposes a king, a "he" in charge of things, which reinforces the status quo and only hints at a more profound problem. "Kingdom" also adopts the language of colonizers. Specifically, the Roman Empire that took the land Jesus stands on. We've already seen Domitian claim that he alone is worthy to receive the kingdom. But even using this word, *basilea*, connotes power, strength, military, and violence. Remember, the Pax Romana, or the peace of Rome, was enforced at the end of a sword. And that sword was often pointed at Jesus' people.

But now, Jesus pairs the language of a kingdom with the imagination of heaven. And for a lot of people, that combination probably worked (at first). They assumed the only way to peace was war. That was the Pax Romana, after all. But not Jesus. He says that the kingdom belongs to the poor in spirit.

People have tried to domesticate this statement. "Well, you see, when he says the poor in spirit, what he really means is those who recognize their need for God." That deadens the impact of Jesus' words though. Poverty of spirit is exactly what it sounds like—those who don't possess what they need, spiritually. You can even see this by jumping over to Luke. There the writer quotes Jesus, "Blessed are you who are poor, for yours is the kingdom of God" (Luke 6:20). Where Matthew hears Jesus addressing spirituality, Luke brings an economic ear to the conversation. Still, both clearly recognize that poverty is not the objective here. Poverty is the context for God's goodness that comes to find us. God cares for those who don't have enough. God searches for those who don't understand. You and I don't want to be poor in spirit any more than we want to be poor economically. And yet God comes for us.

Jesus is talking about the underdogs here. The ones who don't get it. The ones who can't make sense of God.[32] Those who have been left behind by the economics and superstitions of the empire. Jesus says that this new kingdom that he proclaims belongs to—in fact, is built for—them.

And this should have been the moment we knew what Jesus was up to. The construction of a kingdom that opposed the very idea of kingdom. But still, right to the very end, we wanted him to overcome Rome like Rome.

In the throne room, John gives us an image of how our desire for power corrupts our imagination of God's kingdom. Oppression has a way of not only crushing our spirit but also compacting our imagination into imitation. To counter that, John sets our fascination with Roman power against God's character revealed by Jesus. This is, of course, leading to the kingdom imagination Jesus has been talking about all along in the Gospels, but John strings us along by giving us a glimpse of what we think we want: One who sits on the throne in power, and undoubtedly, we are meant to assume this is God from the get-go.

But then John slowly introduces images from Roman cultic practices, melding them with Hebrew worship. Maybe for a moment we begin to wonder about the uncomfortable connections, but the truth is we want a God like this—a God with a kingdom that looks like strength. Ultimately, the question John wants us to face is this—If God is like Domitian, then doesn't that mean empire really is in control? And if God isn't like Domitian, what's the alternative? Domitian doesn't really control destiny, does he? Maybe no one does?

Just as we're ready to despair, and as the scene turns from worship to tears, the Lamb emerges to take the scroll from the one who sits on the throne. The true son who "did not consider equality with God something to be used to his own advantage" (Philippians 2:6), who did indeed ascend to the heavens, but who made himself nothing by taking the very nature of a servant unto death—even death on a cross (2:7–8). God is not like Domitian. Jesus is not like the imperial child. Destiny is not written by the violent.

In self-giving love, Jesus unveils the hidden, authentic history of the world. Faithfulness was not the illusion. Power was. Jesus shows us that God has always been in control. God has always been on the throne; Domitian was never even part of the picture. In fact, for all his pomp and circumstance, Domitian doesn't even deserve mention. He is nothing but whisper and innuendo. Because the control God wields is not rooted in Jupiter's chair; it is found in the sacrifice of the Lamb.

NOTIONS OF POWER

Our whole notion of God being as in love with power as we are strikes me as profoundly myopic. I do get it, though. When you have very little, power is enticing. And when you have a lot, power is intoxicating.

But as a thought experiment, imagine that you had infinite power. Absolute unconstrained power. If that were really true, why would strength matter one whit to you? If that were true, the only thing that would matter, the only thing that would be interesting, would be to give it all away. The only action that an all-powerful God has left is to become weak, and that's the heart of John's throne room vision.

Jesus is Lord not because he can overpower Domitian, but precisely because he is the only legitimate power in the universe that doesn't demand we bend a knee. That's why he alone is worthy in a world with powerful tyrants.

This is not an image of confusion meant to meld Domitian with God. In stark terms, this is John telling us that the emperor is not who he claims to be, destiny is not controlled by the powerful, and it is Jesus who finally unveils God to us. The future, it seems, is written by those who give themselves away.

However, this message was prophetic in another way as well. After Domitian was assassinated in 96 CE, there was a lot of rejoicing that his reign was over. In fact, the Senate passed a decree known as the *damnatio memoriae*,[33] ruling that all statues and inscriptions to Domitian be chiseled away, images melted, and arches torn down. Far from being immortal as he claimed, his legacy was virtually wiped out. Even the name on his neokoros in Ephesus was replaced with that of his father, Vespasian—ironically, a legacy Domitian had tried to diminish.

John's message is that the emperor is not who he is cracked up to be for all his apparent power. He is not a god, not in charge, not in control of your or anyone else's destiny. And God has no need to imitate that broken model of power. Granted, Domitian may sound like a lion. We might even describe his reign as terrifying—but when we finally see power for what it is, it will look like sacrificial love.

LOVE IS AT THE CENTER

So this is how John begins his prophetic view of history. It is not terror, confusion, or bad news; it's not even the apocalyptic desire for violence that we imitate from the empires surrounding us. It is the truth that self-giving love wins. Despite what we may see in the world around us, Jesus unveils the undeniable fact that victory was never about being able to make someone do what you want them to do. That's too shallow a power for one who holds a universe together. Instead, the victory of the Lamb is an apocalypse that dismantles our ideas about power.

The cross revealed that God is worthy of our worship not because God is the strongest, most powerful being in the universe. God is worthy because God looks like Jesus—self-giving love.

For John, it is not enough to trade Domitian for God if we hold on to outmoded ideas of kingdom. The Christ has come. The Lamb has taken the scroll. And nothing will ever be the same again. This one realization does so much to turn so many of our assumptions about God upside down.

Sometimes it's tough to believe that love actually shapes history. After all, millions have died from a deadly pandemic as neighbors chose their individual freedom over their responsibility to one another. Climate change destroys lives and livelihoods worldwide as we pursue short-term wealth over shalom. Our world economy has proven to be inherently fragile. We often choose the politics of partisan corners, refusing to speak honestly and openly with each other. Perhaps it's only natural to look for someone to blame and then call on God to enact justice with a strong arm. We might even be happy with a strongman made of straw to take God's place.

And yet here, with Domitian on the throne, John reveals to us the real danger of empire—that it might slowly infect our imagination until we struggle to explain the difference between God and Caesar. Revelation is not trying to deny your fears or pretend everything is okay. John's not asking us to imagine that our struggles aren't real. He's acutely aware of how hard life can be.

But for John, the universe is full of hope, and he wants that hope to sink deep into our bones. Despite what we might read in the news, at the very center of a rightly ordered universe stands the sacrificial love of the one who came to make all things new, starting with our imagination of power.

The upside-down apocalypse is this: there is more love in the universe than we could possibly imagine, and it's in the Lamb, not on the throne, that we see God fully unveiled.

6

RIDERS OF THE APOCALYPSE

In the last chapter, we saw familiar Hebrew imagery mingled with images of Roman imperial worship. John is calling us to question who sits at the center of our world. Who is really in control of the universe? We know the answer is God, but if our image of God looks like Domitian, does it really matter?

Labels are less important than the images that shape our way in the world, and a God that looks like Domitian will almost certainly shape us in unloving ways. And so we saw the Lamb, looking as if it had been murdered, come and take the scroll from the one on the throne, proving that self-giving love is the only force worthy to direct history. At this, the whole scene erupts into a festival of worship as we see things unveiled for what they truly are.

This is a good start, but there are implications.

SEVEN SEALS AND FOUR RIDERS

> I watched as the Lamb opened the first of the seven seals. Then I heard one of the four living creatures say in a voice like thunder, "Come!" I looked, and there before me was a white horse! (Revelation 6:1–2a)

This is one of the most fertile sections of Revelation for artistic license. The four horsemen have been the subject of very disturbing and, at times, stunning works of art.

For example, as you read you may find yourself picturing the Nazgûl from *The Lord of the Rings*. J. R. R. Tolkien was inspired by the images here in Revelation. Or perhaps for you, it's something more classical. Viktor Vasnetsov depicted the riders of the apocalypse in an 1887 artwork. The Lamb sits at the top of his painting, overseeing the violent destruction brought upon the world. It's a disturbing but strangely compelling work. Maybe you want to go back even further to the Bamberg Apocalypse, an illuminated manuscript of Revelation from the early 1000s CE that depicts many scenes, including the horsemen.

The imagery of the riders of the apocalypse has captured Christian imagination ever since John wrote it down. We have wondered about the meaning, folding it into all kinds of derivative fiction. However, once again, these images do not originate with John. They come from the prophet Zechariah.

> I looked up again, and there before me were four chariots coming out from between two mountains—mountains of bronze. The first chariot had red horses, the second black, the third white, and the fourth dappled—all of them powerful. I asked the angel who was speaking to me, "What are these, my lord?"
>
> The angel answered me, "These are the four spirits of heaven, going out from standing in the presence of the Lord of the whole world." (Zechariah 6:1–5)

And just as John did with the images from Ezekiel, so he now remixes the images from Zechariah for us. In Revelation, the colors are changed up a bit: it's white, then red, then black, then pale, in contrast to Zechariah's red, black,

white, and dappled. John's word for "pale" is a Greek word
that typically means "green." However, it's often associated
with the sick or dead, describing a pale gray.[1] That description
could certainly be appropriate for a dappled horse. And while
Zechariah's vision describes groups of horses pulling chariots,
John's picture is one of singular horses mounted by individual riders. Still, it seems pretty clear where John is getting his
starting point.

What's intriguing is that in Zechariah, these images represent God's action against the Persian Empire in the sixth
century BCE, and that gives us a clue about how John will use
them in Revelation.

THE FIRST RIDER

The first seal is opened, and "there before me was a white
horse! Its rider held a bow, and he was given a crown, and he
rode out as a conqueror bent on conquest" (Revelation 6:2).

In the last chapter, we were given images of the Roman
Empire, strong and imposing, only to have them pulled out
from under us. In the end, the Lamb reveals through sacrifice that the empire wasn't even part of the picture of power.
The surprise is seeing the opposite of what we have been led
to expect.

This time John takes a different approach. The image of a
bow is undoubtedly an image of military power. Nonetheless,
from a scriptural perspective, the use of a bow to denote military might is frequently set at odds with the ability of God
to overcome and bring peace. There is no shortage of verses
where God is said to break the bows of God's enemies (Psalm
37:15; 46:9; Jeremiah 49:35; 51:56; Hosea 1:5). And in Zechariah, where we know John is drawing ideas from, the prophet
uses the same motif to proclaim God's peace to the nations

(Zechariah 9:10). What might surprise you, though, is that in Zechariah it is the battle bow of God's people that must be broken for peace to come. The king anticipated by Zechariah rules without military force.[2] So it is intriguing that Revelation starts this scene using the image of a bow embedded in a picture lifted from Zechariah.

Still, for a rider associated with conquest, Rome has to be at the front of our minds. The Roman armies were fearsome fighting forces; the largest armies in the world today have little on Rome's dominance, which lasted for hundreds of years. Everyone knew to picture Rome if you were talking about conquest in the first century. But this image from John does not look like Rome at all.

Rome didn't use mounted bowmen; they generally used the testudo formation—a row of soldiers holding massive interlocking shields who would advance together toward the enemy, backed up by massive waves of archer fire. They would carry spears for medium-range attacks and short swords for close-quarters combat, and slowly they would inch their way toward the battle.

The use of mounted bowmen, then, was a tactic from outside the empire. If your enemy is better funded and better manned and has more resources than you, you learn to adapt. You don't march yourself at a bigger army; you engage them with small, fast, surgical strikes. You get in, attack a few soldiers, and move out. This is what Rome's enemies had learned to do.[3] In the first-century world, minor tribal powers on the outskirts of the empire would make use of these rapid strikes on horseback. That's what mounted bowmen were used for: to allow underdogs to take on the might of Rome. As powerful as Rome was, the empire still had to spend massive amounts of energy defending its borders from all kinds of pinprick attacks and raids from these smaller forces.

In particular, the Parthians were a painful thorn in the side of Rome. A Parthian shot is the difficult act of shooting an arrow accurately from the back of a galloping horse—something the Parthians were well known for. They lived on the eastern frontier of the empire and were notorious for attacking Roman lands and running away. In his commentary on Revelation, William Barclay writes that "in AD 62, an unprecedented event had occurred: a Roman army had actually surrendered to Volages, the king of the Parthians. The Parthians rode white horses and were the most famous bowmen in the world. A 'Parthian shot' still means a final, devastating blow to which there is no possible answer."[4]

Barclay claims that the Parthians rode white horses. That's probably a bit of a stretch, but we know from records that they prized white or gray horses with black dots, possibly forebears of what we know as Appaloosas today. So an image of a rider with a bow, especially on some kind of white horse, could reasonably be associated with the Parthians. This is not an image of Roman strength like we saw in the last chapter. That myth has already been shattered by the Lamb anyway. This image, attached to the first seal on a scroll that no one but Jesus can open, is an image of profound Roman weakness under attack.

Further, remember that John pulls this imagery from Zechariah, where the riders represent God's action against the Persian Empire of the day. In that case, we should already be clued in that he is probably using the image against the Roman Empire. Armies will always be vulnerable to other armies. Empires will always be a danger to other empires, and this is

John's point. Putting faith in borders to protect us will always have us looking over our shoulders for a new enemy.

THE SECOND RIDER

> Then another horse came out, a fiery red one. Its rider was given power to take peace from the earth and to make people kill each other. To him was given a large sword. (Revelation 6:4)

One of the extraordinary claims of Rome was the Pax Romana. Predominant in all the imperial titles discussed in the last chapter is the central claim that the emperor had brought peace to the world.

Imagine that you lived at that time and an authority came along who crushed raiders and thieves, built you roads—making trade possible—and provided a safe environment to work and live in. Would you really care how they did it? And if they demanded allegiance to the emperor in return, would you balk at the request? Honestly, if he thought himself a god, so long as he kept himself busy in Rome away from your family, would you really worry about his grandiose idiosyncrasies? Truthfully, would any of us object to peace won through the subjugation of others, particularly if it were kept out of sight? Well, this was, for a lot of the public, the very premise of Rome: peace at the point of a sword—as long as it wasn't pointed at you.

We can draw parallels to current foreign policies that claim to work for our best interest while essentially hiding the suffering that our peace demands. We could consider the way our justice systems tilt toward incarceration rather than restoration to sate our lust for revenge. But here John forces the question. What if the borders aren't as secure as you think they are? What if the peace you depend on is not as stable as you have been led to believe? What happens if the sword of Rome is taken away? Does the peace remain? And if not, was it really even peace to begin with?

In Philippians, the apostle Paul quotes a community hymn, writing that at the name of Jesus, every knee should bow and tongue confess (Philippians 2:10–11). It's a famous line, but the quote is far more political than we might imagine—it's an indirect attack on the rule of Caesar, stemming from the fact that the Romans made similar claims about the emperors.[5] For example, the poet Horace writes that "upon you [Augustus], while still among us, we already bestow honors, set up altars to swear by in your name, and that nothing like you will arise after you or has arisen before you."[6] Augustus deserved this honor because he brought peace, but his peace was predicated on war. When Rome invaded a new area, they would bring out all the officials, generals, kings, royalty, influential people, line them up, force them down to their knees, and proceed along the line, asking them to confess allegiance to the emperor. If they said no, they lost their head. If they agreed, they were granted Roman grace. Because this is how the peace of empire works. It is peace or you die; peace at the point of a sword. And at the end of the day, the true religion of Rome, even above the emperor cult, was war, victory, peace, in precisely that order.[7]

Conversely, Paul argues, the Christian story claims that Christ's self-emptying (Philippians 2:6–8) is the source of such worthiness[8]—a narrative we watched play out in the throne room.

So here's the conundrum John is building. If peace is bought at the point of a sword, what happens if that sword is taken away? John argues that if this violently enforced pseudo-peace is taken from the world, people will turn on each other. In fact, violence is what we have been conditioned to do by the Pax Romana.

To dive into the weeds for a moment, this "rider was given power to take peace from the earth and to make people kill each other" (Revelation 6:4). The problem is that the NIV translation is reading too much into a single Greek conjunction.[9] For comparison, the NRSV renders the passage as "[the] rider was permitted to take peace from the earth, so that people would slaughter one another."

That might not sound like a big deal, but it materially shifts the role of the rider from causing the violence to removing the artificial barriers that conceal it. As the scholar David Aune explains, this is "a conscious reversal of the Roman achievement."[10] The rider is John's way of showing the peace of Roman society for the facade that it is. It's always been a fake. This is the kind of peace that comes when a bigger, stronger bully forces you to act in a certain way. Empire can offer us a scapegoat, a common enemy, those outside the walls to focus our anxieties on. But it's still a predatory peace that needs an enemy, and it slowly forms us in its image.

If the walls fall and the pretense fails, then our genuine tensions and conflicts begin to show themselves. The peace of Rome—any peace built on violence—is an illusion after all.

This rider is a statement about war's inability to create shalom.

THE THIRD RIDER

> Before me was a black horse! Its rider was holding a pair of scales in his hand. (Revelation 6:5)

Not only did Rome claim that the peace of Rome was historic, but they also claimed that the prosperity of Rome was unprecedented. To be fair, there was some truth to that. Rome was an economic marvel.

However, when this rider appears we are told that inflation will rise so quickly that staples like wheat and barley will cost a day's wages even though oil and wine will be readily available. This is a strange juxtaposition, with the cost of food reaching crisis levels, suggesting a famine[11] while relative luxuries remain accessible. Granted, rich and poor alike consumed oil and wine regularly (1 Kings 17:12; Lamentations 2:12), but in times of hardship, what are you supposed to do with even small indulgences when it costs an entire day's wages just to buy a loaf of bread?

For reference, this image seems to be drawn from the prophet Joel (Joel 1:10–11). Except in Joel's description of famine, all four goods are diminished as we might expect—everyone suffers. The image in Revelation is twisted, marking with irony how crisis exposes the social inequity around us.[12]

This is about more than a food shortage. This is about the failings of an economic system that disproportionately harms the poor while bringing sustenance to the rich. John tells us that just like our borders and our peace, our prosperity is not what we think it is either. This, too, is predatory. The third rider is a statement about the inability of economic systems to bring equality to the world. You have a good job—that's great. Rome got you work—excellent. There's trade—that's good too. No one can argue that Rome doesn't facilitate commerce. But Revelation asks, Is that really what life is made of? Oil and wine and a nice car to get to a good job? These things are blessings, and we don't need to reject them. But suppose our trust is placed wholly in our bank account and our ability to buy our way out of trouble. In that case, Revelation warns that we will inevitably be caught in the boom and bust of economic instability.

In the present day, the last few years of a worldwide pandemic have brought this home in a new way for many of us. We have seen firsthand how those with the least resources have been most affected by disruptions to the status quo. Wealth affords a certain flexibility to continue drinking our wine within isolated social bubbles while others struggle to work through health risks in order to buy bread to eat.

This image of abundant oil and wine set against unfulfilled basic human needs is meant to unveil the inequity in our prosperity. And if the stability of our society is one economic challenge away from crumbling into chaos, perhaps empire can't create the security it promises.

THE FOURTH RIDER

> Before me was a pale horse! Its rider was named Death, and Hades was following close behind him. (Revelation 6:8)

The death we read about here in Greek is the common word *thanatos*, but here it's used as a title—that's why it's capitalized in English. Hades is used in the same way, even though Hades was not a person in Greco-Roman thought but a place: where the dead await judgment. Here the ideas serve as titles for the rider and a companion. These figures bring with them famine, plague, and apparently wild animal attacks.

This is a complex image to grapple with. Still, the trajectory of the first three riders pushes us to imagine it within a larger sequence. Since death and Hades will ultimately find their fate in the lake of fire (20:13–14), along with all those who destroy the earth (11:18), it doesn't seem reasonable to imagine them as working on behalf of God here. Instead, like the others, it is reasonable to consider that they represent some vulnerability in the structure of Roman society.

A contemporary of John, the philosopher Epictetus, who coincidentally had fled Rome under the reign of Domitian, may provide some help.[13] He wrote the following words while in exile.

> Behold now, Caesar seems to provide us with profound peace, there are no wants any longer, no battles, no brigandage on a large scale, no piracy, but at any hour we may travel by land, or sail from the rising of the sun to its setting. Can he, then, at all provide us with peace from fever too, and from shipwreck, and from fire, or earthquake or lightning? Come, can he give us peace from love? He cannot. From sorrow? From envy? He cannot—absolutely none of these things.[14]

John seems to be on a similar wavelength, arguing again that Rome isn't as impervious as it claims. Armies will always be vulnerable to other armies, and borders are only as secure as the desperation on the other side. Rome can't transform people's hearts, and if the sword goes away, the peace of Rome will fail. Rome can't even guarantee a good economy; it is boom and bust, and those on the margins bear the consequences. Now John orients us to the fact that the social order we depend on has always been impotent to protect us from what really scares us—the things we struggle to explain. Questions like, Why do bad things happen to good people? That's what all these images are about—the profound weakness of life, and it's frightening.

However, once again, it is critical to keep in mind that none of this is the work of God. In the previous scene, the Lamb overcomes through self-giving, which makes him worthy of taking the scroll and opening the seals. But if that scroll represents destiny and a departure from the narrative of Domitian, then the future we are shown now is the fate of all tyrants, including death and Hades. These riders are not meant to be seen as agents of the Lamb carrying out God's plan, as the painter Vasnetsov imagined. They are representative of what happens when our illusions about the world crumble. In revealing God as the one who conquers through love alone, we finally begin to see how our borders, our violence, and our wealth have no ability to save us—how even the powerful are vulnerable to death and confusion.

WHAT WE HIDE FROM OURSELVES

At one point in the gospel of Matthew, Jesus says, "Do not suppose that I have come to bring peace to the earth. I did not come to bring peace, but a sword" (Matthew 10:34). That's always been a troubling passage for me. How can peace embodied in a person claim to bring a sword? But I think I maybe understand that image a little better now.

Our peace is often predatory. Our pseudo-peace depends on borders that keep imagined enemies out and our violence just out of view. Our pseudo-peace is in love with economics, which advantages us but creates an unbearable cost for those lower down the ladder. Our pseudo-peace often requires a villain to point our frustrations at. But for true peace to be embodied in the world, then the pseudo-peace we value has to be torn down.

Jesus drives his point home by quoting from the prophet Micah to describe how fragile our pseudo-peace is. Families can turn on each other and make enemies out of anyone, he suggests (Matthew 10:35; cf. Micah 7:6). Intriguingly, the string of poetry Jesus quotes is partner to an earlier line. The prophet Micah laments that "everyone lies in wait to shed blood; they hunt each other with nets. Both hands are skilled in doing evil; the ruler demands gifts, the judge accepts bribes, the powerful dictate what they desire—they all conspire together" (Micah 7:2–3). Micah's poetry points out that abuse in our social structures creates distrust that moves from our politicians to our neighbors and eventually into our homes. When we welcome the pseudo-peace of the powerful, we undermine the trust we depend on for human flourishing. And Jesus says it all has to come crashing down if we're going to start again.

The sword Jesus brings is precisely the chaos we see embodied in the riders, but this isn't what God does to us. It is the apocalypse of seeing our predation for what it truly is.

The riders are scary, but they are a necessary part of a world set right. Politics, power, economics, and empires turned upside down. These images are meant to unsettle us; hence the drama John chooses to convey. But things are no less dramatic in our personal lives when we truly follow the way of Jesus. The borders of family are blown wide open (Matthew 12:48–50). We are freed from the need for an enemy to know ourselves as loved. Our prosperity is redefined in less individualistic terms, encompassing our neighbor's story. And in all these ways, our comfortable world is destabilized by what is unveiled in Jesus. That's John's point. For things to get better, the apocalypse has to take some things away.

One of the mistakes we can make when reading Revelation is to imagine that John is pointing a finger at a villain rather than revealing something about our world. Conspiracy theories often flourish because they provide us a simple way to explain a problem without the need for self-reflection. John is far too insightful for that. And before we spend our energy searching to identify the riders in our world, we would be wise to consider the ways that Jesus longs to destabilize and restructure the foundations of our lives.

THE FINAL SEALS

So how does this scene end?

When the fifth seal is opened, John sees the souls of those murdered for their faithfulness, and they cry out pleading to be avenged (Revelation 6:9–10).

Trust has been placed in false sources of peace, and it hasn't worked out. The borders were protected at the expense of the vulnerable and still crumbled. Peace came at the point of a sword and prosperity was enjoyed while others went hungry. And all the while, the powers that be preserved security through oppression, turning fury on those who dared put their faith in a better story. People have suffered, so they cry out. The call for revenge is certainly understandable, yet in a puzzling response, these martyrs are given white robes to change into and then asked to wait and watch a little longer (6:11).

Next, a sixth seal is opened, an earthquake shakes the earth, the sun turns black, the moon turns red, and the stars fall from the sky (6:12–13). This is about as apocalyptic as it can get. The imagery here is as if all creation begins to mourn human failures. We have undermined the very premise of creation; God has created this world, and we have broken it with our self-centeredness.

Everyone, all the way from kings down to slaves, runs to hide from the one who sits on the throne and from the wrath of the Lamb (6:15–16)—strong language here designed to send a shiver down even the stiffest spine. This is the end of the world as we know it. The victimization on which our peace rests has been made clear to us, the voices of those we have discarded and blamed have condemned us, creation itself has turned its back on us. In our desperate shame, we expect God to show up like Caesar and punish us. God is here to put down our rebellion with divine anger—the end of all things.

That's the only logical conclusion after all this; the seventh seal means the end. "Who can withstand it?" (6:17).

UPSIDE DOWN

Except that's not what happens.

John writes that he sees another angel, this one with a new seal, God's seal. And the angel calls out in a loud voice, "Do not harm the land or the sea or the trees." Pause the apocalypse until we can put a seal on the servants of our God.

> Then I heard the number of those who were sealed: 144,000 from all the tribes of Israel. (Revelation 7:2–4)

So maybe there is hope! A tiny, righteous remnant has stayed loyal to God through it all. God is going to intervene to save them. Maybe even us if we can sneak our way in. Except that's not what happens either, is it?

Remember in the last chapter when John heard the Lion of the tribe of Judah but turned to see something very different? This time, John hears what he expects to hear, perhaps all that he can muster to hope for right now—a tiny residue of faithfulness that might be saved in the face of God's anger.

Yet when John turns, what he sees is nothing of the sort. Before him is not 144,000 from the tribes of Israel, but a multitude that no one can count, from every nation and language. And all of them are standing before the throne and before the Lamb. They are wearing white robes to symbolize their salvation, they hold palm branches to acknowledge God's sovereignty, and they cry out in a loud voice, "Salvation belongs to our God, who sits on the throne, and to the Lamb" (see 7:9–12).

Do you see what John has done to us again?

We already know that Christ has overcome the world, so this time the pledge, act 1, is an image of Rome's impotence.

Bit by bit and piece by piece, we see that what Rome promises it cannot deliver. A Pax Romana built on violence is destined to crumble eventually. And as we read on, we are implicated in the brokenness of these systems. We are part of the problem, and we deserve to be forgotten. Over the course of six seals, things get worse and worse until we are brought to the point of despair, and we cry out in fear of judgment. The best that even the most faithful among us can imagine is to ask God to avenge them.

But then there's act 2—the turn—a righteous remnant of 144,000—the tiniest of chances that we might escape God's wrath. A lifeboat in a sea of hopelessness.

Yet when we see the prestige and John finally pulls back the curtain on act 3, God's true character is unveiled to us. It is not the retribution that we have expected to witness. It's not even the marginal grace that anyone would have been forgiven for imagining. Instead, in the end, what we see is salvation so great it cannot be counted. We can describe it, we can try to give it a number to make sense of it, but when we actually see salvation for ourselves, it is so far beyond our comprehension it belies belief. God is endlessly good, even in the face of our failings, and that's the point! The apocalypse is not the wrath we have been conditioned to hope for, our enemies punished, and our sins visited upon us. What is unveiled is salvation writ large.

Suppose the throne room scene was meant for churches like Ephesus and Smyrna, churches undergoing persecution who needed to be reminded that God was still in control. If that's the case, the seals are for churches like Laodicea and Sardis. Those that have slowly come to believe they really do have everything they need. That an empire really can provide safety and security under its wing, as long as you keep your head down.

The images here are not meant to reassure us; they are indeed intended to shake us to our core. To jolt us out of the apathy of comfort and reveal to us that even in our well-oiled economies, stable governments, and freedom to worship openly, we still need God to expand our imagination of what is possible. These images are not about terrifying plagues and calamities brought on by a vindictive God. They are about the crumbling of any pseudo-peace predicated on victimization. You don't need to be persecuted in order to identify with these images; in fact, that's not the point. These are images for any of us who have comfortably split our trust between Jesus and empire while someone else paid the price for our complacency.

Maybe we have imagined that we really need someone on the outside in order to feel safe and connected—that borders are an essential part of the human experience. Or perhaps we imagined we could legalize morality to create a better world by forcing Christianity into law at the point of a sword or the tip of a pen. Maybe it's that we have put too much stock in stocks—good retirement plans and well-funded bank accounts—thinking security can be bought. But the Spirit of God would say to us, That peace is fragile, and community at the cost of a victim is brittle.

And maybe this is why we have imagined that God is vindictive and vengeful, looking for the moment to strike us down. We know what our pseudo-peace costs, even if we refuse to look closely. But the upside-down apocalypse is this: our anger at injustice won't reveal God fully; only our love for others can. We can see our structures fall. We can call out and ask God for vengeance. But as John reveals, salvation doesn't belong to us. Salvation belongs to our God. And salvation is better than you think.

Any time you get stuck in Revelation, confused by the images, or concerned about the future—any time you see pain and destruction and you wonder whether you've somehow lost sight of God—turn the page. Because when you are lost, you are where John wants you: primed for Jesus to be revealed.

7

TRUMPETS AND THE TEMPLE

The key to reading Revelation is to bear in mind the concentric circles of Hebrew prophecy. This is how Revelation unfolds: not in linear progressions, but in cycles and repetitions.

By now we should be getting used to John's formula. He builds up an image bit by bit, but just as we get to the scene's climax, he pulls the rug out from under us. That's the nature of this genre-bending prophecy wrapped in an apocalypse. Revelation shows us what we think we want, only to turn it upside down to show us something better.

It's also why we talked about the importance of not getting bogged down in the middle of a scene. When you read, don't stop and let despair get the better of you; wait for the reveal that's coming. In fact, whenever you start to lose hope as you read Revelation, you are precisely where John wants you to be. On the very next page, he will show you just how good, gracious, loving, and self-sacrificing God really is.

When the seventh and final seal is finally opened, "there was silence in heaven for about half an hour" (Revelation 8:1).

This is how the four horsemen of the apocalypse end—not with destruction, but profound goodness. It's almost as if John is saying, "Okay, we've made it to the end of a scene; now pause here, reflect on what you've learned about God. Because we have more to explore."

A FINAL SCENE

There is one final scene in this cycle of Revelation before we witness the enthronement of Jesus for a second time. Starting with that end in mind, notice what happens when the seven trumpets reach their climax.

> The seventh angel sounded his trumpet, and there were loud voices in heaven, which said:
>   "The kingdom of the world has become
>   the kingdom of our Lord and of his Messiah,
>   and he will reign for ever and ever."
> And the twenty-four elders, who were seated on their thrones before God, fell on their faces and worshiped God, saying:
>   "We give thanks to you, Lord God Almighty,
>   the One who is and who was,
>   because you have taken your great power
>   and have begun to reign."
> (Revelation 11:15–17)

Notice anything here? In chapter 1, John calls God the one "who is, and who was, and who is to come" (1:8). Why is God's title shortened here to "the One who is and who was"? Well, in a word, timing. This is an image of God reigning in the world. The end of the story for a second time. God's kingdom has come to the earth.[1]

In Revelation 12, John will start all over again and work his way through the story for one final cycle. He will introduce that story by writing that the time has come for the destruction of that which destroys the earth (11:18), a perfect summary of God's dismantling of evil.

But before we get there, the question is, How did we get here?

REVELATION ACCORDING TO ISAAC NEWTON

There are a lot of different approaches to Revelation, and the trumpet scene gives us an opportunity to consider three of them: the futurist, the preterist, and the literary approaches to the text.

The seven trumpets have been, probably more than any other section of the book of Revelation, fuel for what we sometimes call a futurist reading. This is the idea that each event in Revelation looks forward to some specific event in human history. Most of those events may be in our past, but Revelation is understood to be predicting the future from John's vantage point. This is not a new phenomenon, either; it wasn't invented by *Left Behind*. People have been doing this for centuries.

Isaac Newton, who discovered the laws of gravity and invented calculus (I'd be remiss if I didn't credit Gottfried Leibniz with the co-creation of calculus here) was also an avid amateur reader of Revelation. Six years after his death, his book *Observations on Daniel and the Apocalypse of St. John* was published in 1733. This is just one sentence from the second chapter of that work:

> The whole world natural, consisting of heavens and earth, signifies the whole world politic, consisting of thrones and people, or so much of it as is considered in the prophecy, and the things in that world signify the analogous things in this, for the heavens and the things therein signify thrones

and dignitaries, and those who enjoy them, and on the earth, while the things thereon of the inferior people and the lowest parts of the earth, called Hades or Hell, the lowest or most miserable part of them.[2]

I did not say it was an enjoyable read! But as obtuse as the language is, it lays out Newton's approach to Revelation, which is essentially this: everything you read in Revelation, or "the world politic" as he calls it, must have an analog in history, or "the world natural" as he names it. In other words, everything in prophecy must have a historical counterpart.

This is not to say that Newton takes everything in Revelation literally. When he reads about a beast coming up out of the sea, or a dragon coming upon the land, he doesn't expect to see actual beasts and dragons duking it out. He does believe, however, that these images represent historical events. And perhaps for a guy who taught himself calculus for literally the first time and spent his time crafting the first reflecting telescope to chart the elliptical orbits of the planets, this makes sense. He saw Revelation, and indeed history along with it, unfolding with mathematical precision. If he could observe and predict the movement of a planet, he assumed he should be able to forecast the direction of history by a close reading of Revelation.

Newton saw in the seven trumpets the fall of Rome, the Christianization of the empire, and the adoption of trinitarian thought—which, by the way, he thought was a bad idea. He believed that Revelation predicted the division of East and West during the Byzantine era, and the rise of the papacy in the eighth century. Newton was also not a fan of the pope. He even went so far as to suggest that the end of the age would come to pass in the year 2060.[3] End-times prophecies have come and gone, but Newton's guess is still out there. So who knows!

The point is, a lot of people from many different backgrounds, not just theology, have tried to attach the seven trumpets to historical events. With that in mind, let's walk through a more modern version of this same futurist approach, something you may be familiar with from certain circles in the Christian world.

MODERN WARFARE

Before we look at a contemporary futurist theory, it's important to remember that no one reads Revelation literally. A futurist reading that attaches images to historical events is no more literal than any other approach. Unless we're going to suggest that actual monsters will attack the world, this is all about the interpretation of these metaphors. We all generally acknowledge that John is using apocalyptic symbols here. However, let's imagine for a moment each trumpet as a historical moment.

> The first angel sounded his trumpet, and there came hail and fire mixed with blood, and it was hurled down on the earth. (Revelation 8:7)

Some might theorize that this is an image of the aerial bombings during the Second World War. They could point out that the kind of destruction wrought on Europe during that war was unprecedented in human history. War on that scale had never happened; we had never seen anything like it, but they might say, perhaps John had.

> The second angel sounded his trumpet, and something like a huge mountain, all ablaze, was thrown into the sea. A third of the sea turned into blood, a third of the living creatures in the sea died, and a third of the ships were destroyed. (8:8–9)

This, we could suggest, is an image of the atomic bombs dropped on Nagasaki and Hiroshima. A vision of the mushroom clouds that rose from the bombings. The devastation that happened to the island of Japan.

> The third angel sounded his trumpet, and a great star, blazing like a torch, fell from the sky on a third of the rivers and on the springs of water—the name of the star is Wormwood. A third of the waters turned bitter, and many people died. (8:10–11)

This one, the story might go, is an image of the nuclear meltdown at Chernobyl, the water that poisons people as a reference to radiation. It's said that the name Chernobyl means Wormwood, although there's some debate about that.[4] The specific word here, *absinthos*, refers to a plant called *Artemisia absinthium*, the bitter oil of which was used to treat intestinal worms.[5] The argument has been made that Chernobyl derives its name from the Ukrainian word for wormwood. Ukrainians, though, say no; Chernobyl means "black grass," a reference to *Artemisia vulgaris*, a related but different plant. I don't speak Ukrainian, so I'm not going to weigh in definitively. However, we should acknowledge we are well into the realm of speculative interpretation here when bitter water means radiation poisoning and a star falling from heaven is a nuclear meltdown.

> The fourth angel sounded his trumpet, and a third of the sun was struck, a third of the moon, and a third of the stars, so that a third of them turned dark. (8:12).

This could point to the end of the Gulf War. Iraqi military forces set many oil wells on fire, and it took years to put them out. They billowed thick black smoke into the air, literally blacking out large swathes of the sky.

The fifth angel sounded his trumpet, and I saw a star that had fallen from the sky to the earth. . . . Out of the smoke locusts came down on the earth and were given power like that of scorpions. . . . The locusts looked like horses prepared for battle. On their heads they wore something like crowns of gold, and their faces resembled human faces. (9:1, 3, 7)

This is a famous one. These images have been described as depicting military craft preparing for some kind of future battle. Perhaps the type of aerial strikes needed to carry out a war against small, inaccessible terrorist camps. Some have quickly made the jump from locust to helicopter. Those crowns of gold seen as spinning rotors, scorpions' tails the missiles they fire, and the faces of humans the pilots that fly them.

The sixth angel sounded his trumpet, and I heard a voice coming from the four horns of the golden altar that is before God. . . . The horses and riders I saw in my vision looked like this: Their breastplates were fiery red, dark blue, and yellow as sulfur. The heads of the horses resembled the heads of lions, and out of their mouths came fire, smoke, and sulfur. (9:13, 17–18)

Finally, when this penultimate trumpet sounds, a large army masses, its numbers reaching two hundred million troops (twice ten thousand times ten thousand; 9:16). A fertile mind might conclude that the armored horses breathing fire are an image of tanks massing for a final conflict with God. The colors on their breastplates represent the flags of certain countries. The scale of the army and the combination of red and yellow perhaps point to China as their source.

To be clear, I am constructing this interpretation from whispers and rumors and my own playful imagination. Still, you can see how these ideas take hold and spread.

THE MISSING TEMPLE

As we might now be learning to expect, rather than a final climactic battle, what arrives with the sixth trumpet is a long interlude before the seventh. We already know how the story ends—we read that earlier. Justice comes, God reigns, and the destroyers of the earth are set to be destroyed. But before that, we have two witnesses who come and prophesy on behalf of God in the temple (Revelation 11:3). And this is where all futurist speculation tends to coalesce.

The map I just gave you—World War II, atomic bombs, Chernobyl, the Gulf War, the war on terror, and some unnamed final battle—is only one of many futurist interpretations. For example, Newton saw the trumpets occurring throughout history up until his time in the eighteenth century. And some who write today will see the seven trumpets happening at some future point. Still, the witnesses in the temple are what unites all the speculations.

If you know your history, you know that Nebuchadnezzar and the Babylonians destroyed the first Jewish temple in the sixth century BCE. The second temple was destroyed by Rome when Vespasian sent his son Titus to attack Jerusalem in 70 CE. Since then, there has not been a Jewish temple. In fact, the temple site is currently occupied by the Dome of the Rock, an important holy place in the Islamic faith. It's a beautiful piece of architecture constructed in the seventh century. At its center is the Foundation Stone. This holy site is vital to Jews, Muslims, and Christians because, according to Talmudic scholars, it was the first part of the earth to come into existence when God began to create.[6] The world started with one stone and expanded out into the world around us. And the temple was built where it began.

However, if the witnesses of Revelation 11 are meant to prophesy in the Jewish temple, we have a problem. Not only is there no temple to prophesy in, but the only space where a Jewish temple could exist is currently occupied. No matter how you place the first six trumpets in history, you are stuck waiting for the construction of a third Jewish temple before the story can finish.

This is why you hear all kinds of rumors about the plans for constructing a new temple in Jerusalem. And it is why negotiations between the Islamic authorities that control the Dome of the Rock and the Israeli leaders that govern the city of Jerusalem are followed very closely. For now, at least, we have hit a dead end. We can't get to this final trumpet.

WORSHIP IN THE TRUE TEMPLE

But what if we took a different approach? What if, instead of looking through history, which inevitably leaves us stuck waiting for a temple, we went back and looked at the literary context that Revelation has already handed us? Because if we do, we find that John has already talked to us about the temple of God.

To the church in Philadelphia, John writes,

> The one who is victorious I will make a pillar in the temple of my God. Never again will they leave it. I will write on them the name of my God and the name of the city of my God, the new Jerusalem, which is coming down out of heaven from my God. (Revelation 3:12)

John has already given us an image of God's temple in Revelation. And it is not the temple in Jerusalem; it is the uniquely Christian idea of the temple as the worshiping body of believers. Within the literary context of Revelation, it makes sense

then to think of the temple the way John has already described
it. Not a reconstructed building but the faithful presence of
the Jesus community. We see this in Paul's writings as well: the
temple is us (1 Corinthians 3:16–17).

With that in mind, let's go back and look at this section one
more time, from the start of chapter 8.

> And I saw the seven angels who stand before God, and
> seven trumpets were given to them.
>   Another angel, who had a golden censer, came and
> stood at the altar. . . . The smoke of the incense, together
> with the prayers of God's people, went up before God from
> the angel's hand. Then the angel took the censer, filled it
> with fire from the altar, and hurled it on the earth. (Revela-
> tion 8:2–5a)

Granted, this is a pretty troubling image to launch the
sequence. The prayers of the faithful martyrs are hurled like
fire from heaven at the earth. Rather vengeful stuff to kick
off these seven trumpets. A question, though. Where are these
prayers coming from? Where have we been prepared for
this scene?

For that, we have to go back to something we saw before
the seventh seal surprised us with its pause. If you recall, we
saw those martyred for their faith crying out, asking for vengeance from God (Revelation 6:9–10). It's those prayers that
are now hurled at the world. We asked for violence, and it's as
if God has obliged.

We see fire mixed with blood (8:7), mountains thrown into
the sea (8:8), waters turned poisonous (8:11), and celestial
bodies struck with darkness (8:12). Terrifying insects swarm
(9:3) and an enormous army prepares for battle (9:16). This
entire trumpet sequence is full of violent imagery drawn from
our request for vengeance.

Consider scholar Adela Yarbro Collins's take on this moment. While she agrees that Revelation is ultimately a nonviolent story, she argues that John makes room for what she calls the darker side of human nature.[7] She reasons that giving us a story where all our enemies are killed or tortured or wiped away creates a catharsis for the fact that the world is not what it should be.[8] You could almost imagine a pacifist playing a violent video game to release her frustration before returning to her life of peaceful activism.

The martyrs' prayers go up before God (8:4), and the story begins to play out violent fantasies of what it might be like to wield the power of empire. We're drawn to that kind of imitation. Think of the dominance of superhero films in popular culture. We like to imagine what we might do if we had the power of gods. John indulges our fantasies, piling plague on top of epidemic, as those murdered are promised vengeance seven times over through the seals (Genesis 4:15) and then seven times seven (Genesis 4:24) through the trumpets. We know this story: vengeance needs violence, which only ever escalates. Righteous anger can be intoxicating.[9] But after all that, what do we see? After God takes our advice against the world, what is revealed?

Less than nothing. We see that humankind did not repent. We did not stop worshiping false gods (Revelation 9:20). We didn't walk away from murder, immorality, or greed (9:21). In other words, after all our violent fantasies are allowed to play out, absolutely nothing changes. And this is John's point.

God could send destruction and tribulation. God could take our advice and act like us, and absolutely nothing would change. Because violence is not the god we think it is. It's certainly not the salvation that Jesus reveals.

At this point, six trumpets have sounded. We've seen the solution we wanted, but it hasn't worked. There's been no redemption, no transformation, no repentance. There is no kingdom to speak of. Just more suffering. But the trumpets aren't God's judgment in history. They are here to show us our lack of redemptive imagination as the story turns upside down.

A seventh angel appears, this time holding a little scroll (10:2). John says that this angel gives a loud shout like the roar of a lion, and John is about to write down the thunder he hears (10:3–4). But then a voice from heaven tells him to stop. To seal up what the thunders have said and discard it (10:4). In fact, John is told to take that little scroll and eat it. It will taste sweet in his mouth but sour in his stomach (10:8–10; cf. Ezekiel 2:8–3:3), as if to say that vengeance is satisfying on our lips but destructive once it finds its way into our soul. There are some important signs to pay attention to here. This little scroll (Revelation 10:2, 9–10) is a different Greek word from the one used to describe what we saw in the hand of God earlier (5:1–9). That's an indication that John wants us to mark a distinction. God's worthiness to hold destiny is different from the expectations of vengeance we often grasp tightly.

Second, John tells us that along with the counterfeit scroll he hears a loud shout like the roar of a lion (10:3). And we have heard about a lion before (5:5), only to witness the juxtaposition of seeing the Lamb (5:11; 7:9). The first six trumpets are a divine bait and switch leading to the unexpected mystery that will be accomplished when the seventh trumpet sounds (10:7).

WE'VE SEEN THIS BEFORE

What's fascinating is that we've seen Jesus do something like this before. In the gospel of Luke, as the story is heading toward its climax and Jesus is about to be betrayed, he says to his friends, "If you don't have a sword, sell your cloak and buy one" (Luke 22:36). Which is a hard sell for many who embrace the gospel of peace. Here, though, Jesus is doing something on the slant. Like John, he uses the language of violence to subvert our fantasies about it.

Just moments after Jesus tells his friends to arm themselves, he is arrested, and Peter pulls a sword, attacking one of the men advancing on them. Luke records Jesus yelling, "No more of this!" And then he touches the man's ear and heals him. But then Jesus says something interesting. He turns his attention to those who've come to arrest him, and he says, "Am I leading a rebellion, that you have come with swords and clubs?" (see 22:47–52).

Now, this is a really intriguing moment.

Jesus calls his disciples to get their swords, and then he scolds them for using them. Jesus asks his followers to arm themselves and then seems surprised that the authorities would come armed in the same way. Clearly, there is more to this story than a simple Second Amendment Jesus. What exactly is going on here?

Lots.

First, when Jesus instructs his disciples to purchase weaponry, he quotes from the prophet Isaiah. We've seen him do this before. Here, Jesus quotes from the psalm of the suffering servant, saying that it is written: "He was numbered with the transgressors" (Luke 22:37; cf. Isaiah 53:12). The psalm is one of the most singularly striking passages in the Hebrew Scriptures. It's beautiful. You should go and read the whole thing. I'll wait.

But what Jesus is doing as he applies this imagery to himself is pretty bold. Not just as a claim to messianic identity but also in his conviction that God is never far from us. God has not left anyone to suffer while they wait for justice. God suffers with us—alongside us—numbered with the rebels who struggle for justice.[10] For Jesus, salvation comes not in power or violence, certainly not through war and weaponry, but in standing alongside those who hurt. He even goes as far as to suggest that salvation might, at times, look criminal. Think about that for a second. Imagine Moses standing before Pharaoh, saying, "Let my people go" (Exodus 5:1), or John Lewis getting into good trouble, or perhaps conscientious objectors who refuse their part in war. Throughout history, peace has often been criminalized, and Jesus names this for us here.

All this helps us make sense of Jesus' direction at the start of the passage. Jesus was never interested in a fight. In fact, he shuts that down immediately and heals the one whom his disciple attacks. These swords were never about protection; Jesus refuses to allow them to be used that way. The swords are political theater used to unveil the fact that even though Jesus comes in peace, everyone else, even his friends, want war.

I love the way Joel Green puts it in his commentary on Luke: "The apostles manifest their dullness when they suppose that Jesus opposes his own extensive and emphatic teaching [on nonviolence] by encouraging them actually to possess (or to purchase) weaponry."[11] That's how an academic lays shade, by the way.

The bottom line is that these weapons are here for show. Jesus is making a rhetorical point about the criminalization of peace and the violence that lurks even in those of us who claim the lordship of Jesus.

THE WORD OF WITNESS

If God refuses vengeance, teaching us instead to ignore our revenge fantasies, and if Jesus eschews even self-defense, choosing to unveil the criminalization of peace, what is the alternative? What is the mystery that arrives with the seventh trumpet?

John tells us that two witnesses appear in the temple. They are like the two olive trees of Zechariah (Zechariah 4:11–14). Fiery words come from their mouths, like Jeremiah (Jeremiah 5:14). They have the power to stop it from raining, and they prophesy for three and a half years, like Elijah (1 Kings 17; Luke 4:25). They can even turn water to blood, like Moses (Exodus 7:17). Eventually, the witnesses give their lives for the truth and place their hope in the resurrection the way Jesus does (Mark 8:31). And then, when they are indeed resurrected, John says that "the breath of life from God entered them" (Revelation 11:11), echoing Ezekiel's vision and drawing us back to God's creation (Ezekiel 37:5; Genesis 2:7).

If the first six trumpets represent our thunderous demands for revenge, then the mystery of the final trumpet (Revelation 10:7) is an image of the faithful witness of God's people throughout history. These witnesses that appear in the temple are as deeply metaphorical as the giant locusts and darkened stars of the previous trumpets because they are composite images, pulled from the Hebrew prophets,[12] reminding us that everything points to Jesus.

The mystery of the seventh trumpet—the one that actually accomplished God's purpose (10:7)—is the antidote to the first six. It is the way of Jesus embodied in the people of God.

THE TRUMPETS IN CONTEXT

As intense as the trumpets are, the point is not that God wants to send destruction and tribulation. The point is that no matter how much we want it, vengeance will never lead to God's reign. Revenge is pleasant on our lips, but it corrupts us from the inside. Pain and destruction don't transform people (Revelation 9:20–21). Only grace, witness, sacrifice, truth, and love can do that.

John is hoping that by reading this, instead of being thrown into conspiracies, looking for signs of what's to come, you and I will be implicated in the mission of God's story. God has told us, "I could do all these terrible things, but it won't work. What will is when you go and live the story of Jesus' self-giving. When you do for others what I have already done for you."

So no, the trumpets are not meant to be read as an image of tomorrow, predicting the future for us. Instead, the trumpets are a story intended to point us toward our tomorrows with hopeful purpose. We can change the world.

And this is where those terms I mentioned earlier, preterist, futurist, and literary, collide. A preterist view says all John's prophecy has already happened. Everything you read in Revelation is a description of past events related to the time of John. Certainly, Revelation is a product of a particular time and place, and John is playing with images that need to be understood in his context. We spent a lot of time in chapter 5 making sense of how John uses the reign of Domitian as literary fuel. But the problem with preteristism, as a strict reading, is that it steals John's message from the church. It renders Revelation interesting if we're into history, but it means that for two thousand years since the message was written, we have all been reading a glorified history book. That's not enough for the Christian community that has continued to wrestle with and find hope in these images.

Rome is clearly the context for many of the images that John employs. But Revelation is not about Rome. Revelation uses examples from the powers that surround it, critiquing the particular empire that holds sway, to make a point about the human experience. In the end, every empire, including Rome (and even America), will be nothing but a blip in God's story— an illusion of power—once we see the sacrifice of the Lamb that reveals God's character and kingdom. Rome is nothing but a literary device in Revelation, which is why a purely preterist reading, stuck in the past, won't cut it.

The futurist approach that tries to show contemporary wars or future struggles also steals John's message, though in a different way. It makes Revelation chrono-centric; a story about me and my world and my time exclusively. That can be powerful. It's compelling to think that we live at the climax of history. Yet that arrogance threatens to steal the significance of this book from two thousand years of church thought and reflection. Far too many generations have understood that this book was for them as well. We need something more nuanced.

LITERARY ARTISTRY

We need instead to think of Revelation as literature.

Is John describing elements of the Roman Empire? Yes. Do those same elements rebound throughout human history to be noticed again and again? Absolutely. And this is why every time you awaken to how empire is trying to steal your imagination and make you believe in violence, you have rightly interpreted Revelation regardless of the time period in which you awake. The Apocalypse is about the way that God's character has been shrouded from our view but is now made clear in Jesus. And that is a timeless revelation that we have come back to whenever history repeats.

To rightly talk about the throne room, we have to understand how John contrasts God's worthiness demonstrated in sacrifice against the unworthiness of Domitian enforced through power. We have to keep in mind John's distinction between trusting empire and faith in the living God to understand the seals. To analyze the trumpets, we must hold the futility of vengeance set against the transforming power of Christ's self-giving way. But in each of these scenes Rome is the context, not the story. The story is Jesus alone.

And so the world has become the kingdom of God and Jesus reigns over it all (Revelation 11:15) because this is how Jesus saves our politics. Whenever empire, be that in our economics or allegiance to country, rises up to challenge the peace of God, Revelation is there, whenever we read, to remind us how destructive our fantasies can be. And how graceful the welcome of Jesus truly is.

8

THE NATURE OF EVIL

Christ reigns in the world, and we're only halfway through Revelation. What gives?

In the last chapter, we closed at the end of the second cycle of Revelation. So this means we're about to begin all over again—this time, however, expanding the picture to a view from the cosmos. This is the grand scope of John's imagination: God is not just interested in the church or even the world; God is deeply invested in what it means to repair creation itself. Jesus' final victory is over the anti-God forces of sin and death.

If you've noted how much energy has been put into emphasizing the historical over the theological implications of the upside-down apocalypse, you will see that shift as we move into this final cycle of the revelation because this time around we talk about the nature of evil and the end of death (Revelation 20:14).

FIRST-CENTURY SCIENCE FICTION

The hymn in Revelation 11:17–18 is doing a lot of work. It closes a cycle—declaring Jesus' kingdom come. But it also serves as the mission statement for the next cycle—destroying that which destroys the earth (11:18).

This is vital to the imagination of John. People often assume that Revelation ends in the destruction of the earth, but it's precisely the opposite. As we read, we need to remember that God is firmly on the side of creation in this book. God is here not to destroy the world but to work against the forces that threaten God's good work. That's the version of the story we are about to begin now.

> Then another sign appeared in heaven: an enormous red dragon with seven heads and ten horns and seven crowns on its heads. Its tail swept a third of the stars out of the sky and flung them to the earth. (12:3–4)

So far, most of the imagery in Revelation has been drawn from human experience. Even the four horsemen of the apocalypse are fairly accessible images—mean men on nasty-looking horses, granted—but we can picture these figures in real life.

Now we've turned a corner. The scope of the story has expanded, and so have the images. We are introduced to a great red dragon. In the next section, we will be introduced to a pair of beasts and a figure named Babylon who rides on the back of the dragon, drunk on the blood of martyrs. We are well out of the realm of everyday human experience here! In fact, we are firmly in the category of what we might call first-century science fiction.

This alternative way of seeing the world is part of the appeal in Revelation. Think of *Star Wars*, or *The Matrix*, or whatever sci-fi film you love right now. These types of movies have very little in common with our surface experience of the world. Yet we're drawn to them because the writers find a way to weave human emotion into the midst of fantastic images. Our familiar hopes and fears placed in unpredictable settings is part of how the stories speak in compelling, even surprising ways. If John were writing today, I could imagine Revelation with robots.

Larger-than-life characters, whether the dragons of ancient mythology or the light saber–wielding warriors of modern sci-fi, take our experience of the world and extrapolate it out to the furthest reach of our imagination. Evil becomes a multi-headed beast. Goodness becomes a star-spangled Avenger. The bad guys get more villainous, and the heroes become more heroic. This is just the fiction of the day.

However, this shift in imagery also signals a shift in story-telling. In Revelation, we've seen evil infect the world, and it is scary: the oppression born of economics and politics harms us profoundly. But now John wants to talk about the nature of evil itself. And the only way to do that is to make the story so big and the villains so bad that it becomes unmissable. These images we're about to encounter are no more bizarre than those in any movie at the local cineplex. The question is, What do these images tell us about our world?

THE MYTH OF LETO

To live under Rome was to live in one of the most multicul-tural milieus in human history. We often think of our cities as becoming very multicultural, and to an extent they are, but by that we mean that different ethnicities live together within a certain proximity. However, as a white Christian who grew up in Canada, I am well aware that as part of the dominant culture, there has never been a lot of pressure on me to learn the stories of my neighbors.

In Rome, a lack of cultural curiosity wasn't really an option. Not only were there different languages, but there were also different religions, politics, cultures, and economic strategies interacting daily. A saying passed through the Jewish communities of Rome that you learned Hebrew for worship, Aramaic for conversation, Greek for trade, and Latin for politics. The idea of a monoglot was absurd in Rome.

And that cultural sharing also became embedded in how Christians talked about their story. After all, if you wanted to make a point about your god, you would want, you might even need, to tell that story using multiple cultural touchpoints. And we've seen John do this throughout the book of Revelation. He has borrowed images from Hebrew worship and the imperial cult. We've seen Revelation use pictures drawn from the narrative of Rome and threats to the Pax Romana. Here, though, we are reading from a new source—the retelling of a Greek myth—the story of Leto.[1]

Here are the Coles Notes (or CliffsNotes, for those south of the border). The god Zeus comes down to earth and meets a woman named Leto. Infatuated, he has sex with her, and she becomes pregnant. Zeus's wife Hera is incensed by this and plots against Leto. Leto, however, is pregnant with twins, the gods Apollo and Artemis. These children go on to play central roles in the Greco-Roman pantheon. Apollo was variously recognized as the god of sun and light, the god of truth and prophecy, the god of healing and plague, and music, and poetry. As the son of Zeus, he wore many hats. However, his most famous title was one that might sound familiar—the Light of the World. Emperor Nero even styled himself in the role of Apollo,[2] similar to how Domitian took on the guise of Jupiter. Artemis was also significant, known as the goddess of the hunt, wild animals, wilderness, childbirth, and virginity. She, too, had a lot of roles.

The story goes that while Leto is in labor, a great snakelike dragon named Python (pronounced "pee-thon") is sent by

Zeus's wife Hera to devour the babies. To say she is not pleased with her husband's philandering would be an understatement.

The dragon, however, was not unique to the story. This monster was a ubiquitous figure in ancient mythologies, showing various forms across many cultures to represent chaos. The Babylonians called him Tiamat. The Hebrews called him Leviathan. The Greeks called him Python.

The great dragon sent by Hera crouches down in front of Leto to eat her children as they are born, but just when the babies are delivered, Zeus steps in to snatch them up to Olympus with him. There he gifts each of them a special arrow.

Artemis uses her arrow to become the goddess of the hunt and wild animals; Apollo stays in Olympus for three and a half years, or 1,260 days (cf. Revelation 12:6), and grows into a man in that time. He's a god, so normal rules don't apply. But once fully grown he takes his arrow and comes down to earth to fight the forces of chaos. Apollo confronts Python, kills the dragon, and ushers in a new era of peace and prosperity for humanity. You can see why Nero wanted to be associated with such fun.

Now, this story comes to us from Greek mythology, but the Romans loved these tales. They adored Greek culture, and they talked about the empire and the emperor as the embodiment of Apollo all the time. Their version went like this: The emperor was the one who fought back against the forces of chaos embodied by all those outside the borders trying to undo the peace of Rome. The emperor was there to bring peace and prosperity to the world, just like Apollo. And indeed, the emperors often called themselves saviors of the world, sources of light, bringers of peace. All of this was done in the spirit of Apollo.[3]

So once again, we find John using conventional imagery. Anyone living under Rome would have immediately recognized this story.[4] Interestingly, John also has a compelling parallel to draw from in the Hebrew Scriptures. Psalm 74 hints at the story of a divine hero battling the dragon of chaos,[5] and the Scriptures also depict Israel as a woman in labor, just like Leto (Isaiah 26:17; 66:7; Micah 4:10). These images were sometimes connected to Israel waiting for the coming Messiah who would save the world (Isaiah 49:6).

THE BATTLE IN HEAVEN

In John's version of the myth, the great red dragon is Satan, the personification of all that opposes God (Revelation 12:9), the woman is the people of God, and the child is the Savior we have been waiting for. There are differences in the narrative, though.

As soon as the child is born and snatched away to safety, a battle erupts as heaven goes to war with the dragon. The dragon loses this war, as expected, and is cast down on the earth. Notice, though, that instead of a magical arrow, the triumph comes very specifically through the blood of the Lamb and the word of testimony (12:11).

As we saw in the last chapter, hearts are changed not by thunder and pain but instead by the witness of those who embody the peace of Christ. Here, John once again refuses to resolve the battle in brutality. Instead, the dragon is overcome by the nonviolence inspired by the way of Jesus.

In this story, the child saved from the jaws of the dragon is indeed the savior of the world,[6] but Jesus does not ascend to his Father, returning with a weapon like Apollo; this child instead rouses an "army" of peace that overcomes through self-sacrifice. In fact, once the dragon realizes that this army isn't interested in fighting back, he concedes he has no power over them and leaves. We read, "Woe to the earth and the sea, because the devil has gone down to you! He is filled with fury, because he knows that his time is short" (12:12).

And this is an interesting moment. We see the dragon "hurled down" (12:10) when John is leaning into our battle fantasies born from the myth of Apollo, but then he switches to the image of the devil leaving heaven (12:12) once the nature of that victory is made clear.

A central claim of Revelation is that Jesus turns our stories upside down, including our myths about redemptive violence. In this climactic confrontation, God does not meet evil with opposing malice. God inspires an aikido-like subversion that leaves evil powerless.

I love this image. Pastor and theologian Gregory Boyd writes about it in his book *The Crucifixion of the Warrior God*. There he describes aikido as "a martial arts technique that trains 'warriors' to engage in nonresistant combat, turning the force of aggressors back on themselves in order to neutralize their opponent and hopefully to enlighten them regarding the evil in their heart that fueled their aggression."[7] Suppose the dragon's power over us is the ability to keep us trapped in cycles of violence, thinking that we must constantly look for a new enemy to cast out in order to preserve our peace. In that case, it's only in refusing to "fight" that we can ever escape the dragon's grip.

Think about it this way, Satan doesn't care whom you fight as long as you define yourself by the fight. Fight him; he wins. Notice him goading you into a war and turn your violence toward another; he still wins. Evil is defined by how it moves us to destroy God's creation, including our neighbor, rather than by any of the particular battles we engage in.

This is what Jesus illuminates on the cross, and it's what John wants us to see here. Evil is defeated only when we refuse to fight violence with violence. The cross overcomes evil precisely because it is the subversion of all our Apollo-like myths that keep us fighting.

There's a fascinating moment in the Gospels when Jesus asks, "How can Satan drive out Satan?" (Mark 3:23–26; Matthew 12:26–27). The antagonists in the encounter have accused Jesus of expelling demons through the power of Beelzebul. It's a tense moment (see Mark 3:22). That somewhat counterintuitive accusation of expelling demons through the power of Satan[8] seems to have been a typical charge against those one didn't like.[9] Still, it was emotionally charged language. If you assume God is on your side, and that anyone not on yours is on the side of evil, you can justify a lot of bad behavior. Jesus, however, quickly flips this back on his detractors, pointing out the flaws in their logic. Why would Satan help me defeat Satan?

This is more than just a witty response. It's an invitation to reconsider our underlying assumptions about the world. When we view life in purely oppositional terms, we misunderstand the nature of evil, and Jesus invites us to reconsider our assumptions.

If I drive out demons by the power of Satan, doesn't that mean Satan opposes himself and is already defeated? No, says Jesus, to our surprise. The NIV translates the start of Mark 3:27 with the injunction "in fact," but that's a bad translation. The word *alla* means "on the contrary."[10] In other words, Jesus is about to offer an alternative explanation.

What if Satan doesn't care about sides so long as we keep finding someone new to fight? What if Satan will gladly drive out Satan if it means we discover a new adversary to hate?

After all, in that case, Satan still runs the show. Jesus says, Your accusation is flawed, but more importantly you have missed the way that evil anchors its hooks in you. Satan is only truly defeated once we sneak in and take away his power over us because the way to bind Satan is to refuse to play his game (see 3:27).

As human beings we are inherently defined by our need for an enemy. It's how we define ourselves, it's how we police the boundaries of our social groups. But the cross is the dismantling of this ethos. We push Christ away. We scapegoat him in the most egregious display imaginable and yet he forgives us still. In that moment, all our illusions about divine violence should have been disarmed as we saw God for who God truly is—the one who absorbs and transforms rather than demands violence. This is God's victory over evil.

As much as I love a good Marvel movie, our popular stories of the heroes' triumph through violent strength have malformed our imagination of victory. God intends not only to win, but to turn our love of war upside down. And for John, it's these juxtapositions that are key. The way of Jesus supersedes the war of Apollo and the terrifying dragon that is ultimately impotent in the face of self-sacrifice. That's what John wants us to see by turning the myth of Apollo on its head.

Satan wasn't overcome with swords and spears. That kind of victory would have only transferred our hate onto someone new. John reminds us that Jesus was victorious when he was snatched from the cross to heaven, that the dragon was defeated by the power of nonviolent testimony, and that we participate in this story when we refuse violence as the means to our end. We reject the defanged destroyer, and in that, we disarm evil's power over us for good.

THE WAR ON EARTH

Having been defeated by the nonviolence of heaven, the dragon goes down to the earth raging with fury (Revelation 12:12). He goes to war on the woman. He chases her, but she flies to safety. Then he spews a torrent of water from his mouth, but this time the earth opens up and swallows the water to protect her. This is a subversion of the image we saw in Revelation 6:12–13 when we imagined creation turning against us. Now we see that all of creation is united in nonviolent opposition to evil. Finally, the dragon goes off to attack the woman's children, attempting to goad them into the kind of war he couldn't provoke in heaven.

The dragon goes to the edge of the sea and calls forth a beast with seven heads and ten horns, a monster that represents politics and empire. He also calls for a beast from the land that looks like a lamb but speaks like a dragon, representing religion and deception. There's also a harlot drunk on the blood of the oppressed, a figure that represents the economics of slavery and subjugation. We'll explore these characters in detail in the next chapter, but for now I want to focus on two points that John is making here.

First, the systemic oppression revealed in the last cycle should not be overlooked. Yes, systems are manifestations of human sin, but those systems are also very literally the servants of the very evil that Jesus defeated on the cross. You cannot be anti-Satan without opposing systems that oppress.

Second, John wants us to understand that all this raging and roaring and attempted war-making is a proof that evil has become utterly impotent in the light of Jesus. The only strategy that evil has left is to get you to forget the way of peace.

Now, I understand that at first blush, the image of a dragon flanked by beasts and terrorizing the faithful is scary. Even if we realize that these characters represent politics, religion, and economics, to see them used against us is frightening. But ultimately, that's not John's goal. He's not trying to intimidate you into submission. He's trying to demonstrate how desperate and fragile evil has become.

In the story of Leto and Python, Apollo makes war on the dragon. He attacks and overcomes Python, thereby bringing light to the world. In the ancient Babylonian tale, the hero Marduk attacks the dragon Tiamat, slaying her and using her corpse to hold back the waters of chaos. In the Roman version, it is the empire who battles for control of the borders, pushing back the invaders and bringing peace to the earth. But all these myths only serve to make us more dependent on violence and more fearful of what an enemy can do to us.

Jesus' is an entirely different image of victory; one grounded in nonviolence. In John's version of this story, just when the dragon thinks that it has won, the child is snatched up to heaven (12:5). That word "snatched" in Greek is the word *harpazo*. It's connected to the English word *harpoon* and can be translated as "grabbed" or even "stolen." Jesus uses an adjectival form of the word to describe "the rapacious ravenousness of wolves"[11] (see Matthew 7:15). But John uses such an evocative word here because what he has in mind is Christ's death. This harpooned child evokes the Lamb who was slain—Christ nailed to a cross—with evil about to devour him. And just when the dragon believes it has him in its teeth, Christ is snatched away to heaven in his death. In John's imagination, Christ's weakest, most vulnerable moment—his greatest sacrifice—is his overcoming glory. At that moment, evil was done for. And the dragon is filled with fury because he knows his time is up (Revelation 12:12).

The irony of this dragon image is that despite its scale (pun intended), the narrative is not about the strength of evil at all. It's the story of a caged lion. John is saying, "Yes, I get it—there's evil in the world, and sometimes it looks scary, like a monster, even. I know it feels like evil wars against you, and it hurts. I know that you struggle to trust that there is good in the universe because of what is happening around you. But believe me, evil is not as strong as you think it is. In fact, the reason that evil roars is because the story is over."

9

MONSTERS ATTACK

As we begin this chapter it might be helpful to talk for a moment about authorial intent in the scriptures. We are about to encounter some enigmatic figures, but John is also going to present us with riddles to solve surrounding their identities. Some of the questions we can ask when dealing with such puzzles are, Who is speaking here? Is this John writing to us, or is God speaking? Does John know the answer to these riddles, or does it even matter whom John thought these visions represented?

In my view, it absolutely does matter whom John thought he was talking about. All Scripture, including Revelation, is the product of a partnership. And as mysterious as that partnership is, the fact that John is contributing to the story we read is significant.

One of the best metaphors to imagine the nature of the Scriptures is the incarnation. As Christians, we affirm that Jesus is at once both fully human and fully divine. Yet, somehow, there's no contradiction in that for us. Granted, it gets complicated, and we continue to wrestle with the implications of that conviction. But we trust that the mysterious interaction of the human and divine is an essential part of faith.

Are the Scriptures a human product? Sure, they are. The Bible is a collection of reports documenting humanity's experience of God throughout history—all the things we get wrong and some of what we get right. But does that mean the Scriptures are not divine? Of course not. The Scriptures recount exactly the story that God wanted to tell. The story that leads us, inevitably, to Jesus.

This approach to Scripture means that when we read a prophecy in the Bible, even a vision like the one captured in Revelation, we are listening in on a dialogue between a human being and the Spirit of God. John is a human person in a particular time and place, with a posture, culture, and language that limits him. And yet he is interacting with the Spirit, who invites him to see his world from a larger, more beautiful perspective. For that invitation to have meaning, it must be filtered through an experience that John understands, and for that narrative to make sense, it has to be filtered again through language that John's audience comprehends.

This adds another layer of complexity for you and me, who come along some two thousand years later and may not be familiar with first-century metaphors. But all of this is an essential part of the beauty of the Scriptures. Not simply that they speak for God, but that they show us the divine in dialogue with God's people. This, too, is part of the message of Scripture.

With that in mind as we encounter these figures and the riddles that surround their identities, the way to approach this is not to imagine that John is as confused as we are by what he writes—to think that we can drop in any identity that makes sense to us no matter how absurd it would have been to John. That approach reduces the human person John to a glorified stenographer instead of the partner that God chose for this revelation. Instead, these riddles are designed to invite, compel, maybe even force the reader to engage what God has made clear to John. Make no mistake, John wants us to wrestle with these questions, but he knows exactly what he's trying to say.

ANOTHER SEVEN

So far, we have encountered seven seals and then seven trumpets. Over the next two chapters we will explore a section known as the seven bowls of wrath.[1] In some ways, you can take these seven bowls and line them up with what we have read before, mapping the first seal to the first trumpet and to the first bowl. And while it is true that Revelation speaks in cycles, repeating stories and themes for effect, that kind of strict correlation between the three sections is probably taking things too far. John is giving us literary retellings with each new perspective, and therefore the images serve different purposes each time.

In the seven seals John is illustrating how the claims of imperial destiny are undone by the self-giving of the Lamb (see chapter 6 of this book). In the seven trumpets, we witness how our vision of retribution is overcome by the grace of Jesus (see chapter 7). Now, in the seven bowls, we see God's wrath poured out on that which destroys God's creation (Revelation 11:18). It's crucial to note here that the object of God's wrath in this final section is not creation itself. It is those anti-God forces of sin and death that serve evil and tear at what God has made. This is why properly solving John's identity riddles becomes paramount.

Still, the fall of empire, the salvation of creation, and the end of destruction are not competing agendas. They are the same victory of Christ narrated from three different vantage points.[2] However, because there is a new objective in each telling, the story takes on new forms.

THE BEAST FROM THE SEA

We are first introduced to the beast from the sea. This is the passage in Revelation most often associated with the antichrist, and there are a few reasons why. This beast is given power and authority by the dragon. This beast has seven heads, one of which suffered what appeared to be a fatal wound that has since been healed. And on those seven heads are ten horns and crowns. People start to worship both the dragon and his emissary the beast, and they ask themselves who could ever wage war against such a powerful force. Eventually, all authority over every tribe, people, language, and nation is offered up to this monstrous beast (Revelation 13:7), and that line should give us pause. Where the beast conquers every tribe, people, language, and nation, the Lamb redeems. This beast is literally the anti-Jesus.

And this is precisely how the term *antichrist* is used elsewhere in the Christian Scriptures. In 1 and 2 John, the writer talks about anyone who opposes the way of Jesus as antichrists (1 John 4:3; 2 John 7). You can be anti-Christ when you choose violence to achieve your ends. I can be anti-Christ when I allow greed to overwhelm my commitment to neighbor. More importantly, a system can become anti-Christ when it is elevated above the needs of God's children. Policing that prefers to protect existing structural imbalances over the ongoing pursuit of justice, or an economic policy that prioritizes gross domestic product over the wellness of human persons—these, too, are anti-Christ. The term is not a title. It is a description of the way we choose to live in the world. It might be surprising to realize that the word *antichrist* never shows up in the book of Revelation. Only the descriptions of actions that counter the way of Jesus.

Still, this first beast is diametrically opposed to the way of Christ. The beast embodies an ethic counter to the peace of Jesus. Therefore, this figure is anti-Jesus. We should not, however, be looking for the beast's identity in a particular villain. That is not the intent of the image, as John is about to make clear.

This beast has seven heads, ten horns, and ten crowns (Revelation 13:1). This depicts it as exceedingly powerful. Crowns associated with horns instead of heads might seem odd at first, but it is likely meant to emphasize that the beast's prestige comes through brute force and intimidation.[3] Another contrast with the Lamb.

We're also told that this beast looks like a leopard but has the feet of a bear and the mouth of a lion. This imagery, as bizarre as it sounds, is another set pulled from the Hebrew Scriptures. Specifically, it comes from Daniel's vision of four successive beasts. The first is a lion, the second is a bear, the third is a leopard, and finally, a ten-horned monster (Daniel 7:3–7). Sounds familiar, right? For Daniel, these villains represent successive empires: the Babylonians, the Meads, the Persians, and the Greeks.[4] Here, John has taken all these images and combined them into one great beast—the anti-Jesus, violence-wielding embodiment of empire.

But we're not done. Because John has also added the image of seven heads, one of which was fatally wounded but appears to be alive (Revelation 13:3). He has also given this beast a number, which is 666 (13:18). And all of this points us to Nero.

CONSPIRACY THEORIES

Nero lived before the time Revelation was written and is famous for being a bit of a loose cannon. He was the last emperor of what is called the Julio-Claudian dynasty. In chapter 5 of this book, we met Domitian, the sixth and final emperor in the Flavian dynasty that followed.[5] And if we were to take Nero as the first and begin counting, Domitian would land us at seven.

But Nero was the source of some tall tales himself. During his reign, a great fire destroyed much of Rome in 64 CE.[6] Because the fire was widely attributed to Nero,[7] a scapegoat was needed to deflect the blame, and the early Christian community provided an attractive solution.[8] Nero pointed a finger at the Christians for angering the Roman gods by not honoring them sufficiently, and many Christians were martyred during this period.

In the end, however, Nero died by suicide.[9] This was a problematic ending for the son of a god. The result being that very few people, not even senators, were allowed to see his body. And rumors developed that Nero hadn't died at all but had gone into hiding and would eventually return to take control of Rome.[10]

Centuries later, Augustine wrote that some believed Nero "now lives in concealment in the vigor of that same age which he had reached when he was believed to have perished and will live until he is revealed in his own time and restored to his kingdom."[11] This conspiracy theory took hold in the popular imagination and became known as the Nero *redivivus* legend. A dead emperor who would return. It's hard not to see this story in John's language of the fatally wounded and yet healed head.[12]

To be clear, though, John is talking about the nature of evil, not Nero. He's already shown us that this beast is a conglomeration of all the empires that have come before, so this is not even about Rome per se. Not for a second did John believe Nero would return from death—only the Lamb can accomplish that. What John recognizes in this wild conspiracy theory is a more profound truth. When it comes to the purposes of evil, people, even emperors, are disposable. When one head of state is cut down, another is there to grasp at power. When one empire falls, another rises to impose its will. The dragon doesn't care about Nero or Rome or Domitian or America. Only that violence reigns. This is why attacking the beast to chop off a head is a futile strategy. Only refusing the dragon's war can undo his tools.

John's intent here is to say that if you want to see what empire really looks like, to see just how grotesque and evil this beast can be, then all you have to do is remember what it was like under Nero. The irony is that by combining the Nero *redivivus* legend and the successive empires of Daniel into one monster, John is actually throwing shade at Rome. This present empire is nothing more than another weapon for an impotent dragon trying to draw us into a fight he's already lost. Rome is a pawn.

And then John doubles down.

THE MARK OF THE BEAST

> This calls for wisdom. Let the person who has insight calculate the number of the beast, for it is the number of a man. That number is 666. (Revelation 13:18)

Ancient Greek and Hebrew didn't have symbols for numbers. Certain letters were assigned different numeric values—think Roman numerals. In Hebrew, numbers were assigned to the alphabet from one to nine by ones, then ten to ninety by tens, and one hundred to nine hundred by hundreds. Since this is how numbers were written, the practice of assigning a numerical value to a word became popular as well. This practice was called gematria. The Greeks did it too, but called it isopsephy.

Now, since John employs this enigmatic number, many people have used all kinds of bizarre machinations to make

666 equal pretty much anyone they want. Ronald Wilson Reagan—6 letters, 6 letters, 6 letters: antichrist! One of the characters in the novel *War and Peace* finds a way to make Napoleon equal 666. Antichrist! I have no doubt people are working right now to make whoever is president at the time you read this equal 666. There is actually a diagnosed phobia called hexakosioihexekontahexaphobia—fear of the number 666.

However, the best evidence we have that John has Nero in mind with 666 is that very early manuscripts of Revelation vary and offer two different numbers. Some say 666; some say 616. In fact, our earliest manuscripts of Revelation say 616. Bible translators know this,[13] but because 666 is so iconic, no one wants to change it in our English Bibles.

Here's the thing: Nero can be spelled two ways. The first is a Hebrew pronunciation, Kaiser Nerone, which adds up to 666. The second is the Greek pronunciation, Kaiser Nero, which adds up to 616. The point is that John's meaning was so clear that scribes who were more familiar with a particular pronunciation of Nero's name took it upon themselves to add up the numbers differently to get the point across. In other words, absolutely everyone in the first century knew exactly whom John was talking about here.[14]

One final connection to the number 666. In the book of 1 Kings, we are told that the weight of gold that Solomon's empire brings in every year is 666 talents, amounting to about twenty-three metric tons (1 Kings 10:14). To say it differently, a lot of gold. If we are purely talking about objective measurements of gold, it's quite a coincidence to see 666 pop up all the way back in 1 Kings. Objective is probably not the right way to think of this measurement, though.

In Hebrew literature, numbers often convey meaning. We see this in Hebrew gematria. Since creation culminated in six days of work and a seventh day of rest, the numbers six and seven were significant. Seven was often associated with completion. Think of all the sevens we have already encountered in Revelation. Six, on the other hand, was associated with toil and work. Therefore, when we read 666 in 1 Kings, it should at least make us wonder about the larger narrative—what is it that leads us to this impressive but disconcerting haul?

We can answer that by backing up a couple of chapters. In 1 Kings 9, we read how Solomon built his empire (9:15). The euphemism "forced conscripted labor" might serve to obscure the reality, but no matter how you say it, Solomon used slaves to build his military bases at Hazor, Megiddo, and Gezer. At the height of Israel's power, Solomon used slavery to build his military might. And this after God repeatedly reminded the Israelites not to oppress their neighbors, for they were once outsiders themselves (Exodus 22:21; 23:9; Leviticus 19:34; Deuteronomy 10:19; 23:7; 24:22). If our Spidey-senses aren't tingling already, we also read that Solomon built up massive armies (1 Kings 10:16–17), importing horses from Egypt and Kue and chariots from Egypt, and then exporting them to the Hittites and the Arameans (10:28–29).

This means that Solomon sold weapons to other Canaanite kingdoms to fund his ongoing wars. In other words, Solomon, who was supposed to usher in an era of peace after David, became an arms dealer and a merchant of war. The writer of 1 Kings, who is generally quite critical of the monarchy, says that the wealth Solomon accumulated was 6—6—6, work—work—work, evil—evil—evil. John picks up on this and says it's even worse than you can imagine—wealth and power and politics are a deadly combination no matter where they show up—Israel, Rome, or otherwise.

From here we can also see why this mark is associated with buying and selling in John's imagination (Revelation 13:17)—the greed that showed up in Solomon was now manifest in the emperor's visage stamped on every coin in one's pocket. You literally could not buy or sell in Rome without acknowledging an economy that worshiped the emperor. Underwhelming as it may be for conspiracy fanatics, the mark of the beast is probably as simple as that. Our love for money reinforces the power that empires hold over us.[15]

Once again, it would be much easier if John were describing some vast global conspiracy where elites plot to control us, but the truth is simultaneously more mundane and insidious. We benefit from the systems that oppress God's creation, and we are marked by that participation. We buy and sell, slowly coming to believe that our well-being is tied to the success of the empire.

Realistically, what can we do? Do we stop using money? Well, that may well be what John is advocating. A return to small integrated communities founded in the pursuit of mutual economic good. Still, regardless of the specific era we live in, the challenge is to resist empire's desire to control our imagination. Empire wants nothing more than for you to believe that nothing can change and that tomorrow can only be an increased expression of today—good as defined by Caesar. But "we will never embrace [John's] ethic of succession until we cease to be comfortable in the empire."[16] And that starts with acknowledging how profoundly our imagination of the good life is shaped by money and then actively rejecting how deeply our politics are contoured by economics.

Again, to be clear, this last cycle is about the nature of evil and the multitude of ways it sneaks into our lives. The beast is not Nero, and the mark is not a Roman coin. Remember, there are seven heads, and even when we think one dies, another will rise to take its place. The beast is a representation of power—the way empire tries to dominate our imagination of what is possible.

For all empire's claims to virtue, from the Pax Romana to the city on a hill, empire's commitment to power means it can only serve as a pawn in the larger struggle of God and evil.

THE BEAST FROM THE LAND

The beast from the land (Revelation 13:11–17) looks like a lamb but sounds like a dragon. And that juxtaposition draws our imagination back to the Lamb that was slain from Revelation 5. There we expected to see a warrior lion but were shaken by the image of a victimized Lamb. Here, this figure draws us in with its placid appearance but then betrays its true character. If the first beast was the anti-Jesus, this beast is the counterfeit Lamb. And it uses deception to encourage people to worship the first beast. This beast represents religion that cosigns the objectives of politics. It may dress in the guise of peace and take on the language of worship, but the object of its fervor is power.

And that objective—the worship of empire—is filled with camouflaged violence. Religion often seems benign for those who remain in its good graces. It's only when we step outside the status quo that we uncover the violence we have suppressed. As we saw with the seven seals, politics is often able to hide its violence from our view. A peace predicated on crushing difference and scapegoating outsiders can easily become justified as a necessary evil. But in a similar way, religion that reinforces such boundary keeping plays the same role—covering up our misdeeds. This is why it's only in listening to the voices that come from outside the privilege of power, both politically and religiously, that we are able to realize that our peace is often predatory. There is a difference between keeping the peace that is already in place, already disadvantaging some, and making peace in the model of God's upside-down kingdom. That kind of peacemaking will almost always find itself at odds with power (Matthew 5:9).

In this worship of the first beast, the second's identity is made clear—any religion that uncritically reinforces political hegemony. In chapter 5 of this book, we saw the specific religion of the imperial cult and the worship of Domitian that followed from it. Here John reminds us that every empire has priests who serve to sanctify its violence. And that religion itself can be co-opted into just another tool for the dragon.

It looks peaceful, it might even accomplish nice things, but any religion that provides cover for the violence we don't want to see is anti-Christ.

THE WOMAN CALLED BABYLON

BABYLON THE GREAT
THE MOTHER OF PROSTITUTES
AND OF THE ABOMINATIONS OF THE EARTH.
(Revelation 17:5)

Finally, we reach the woman called Babylon, who also comes with a riddle. This one is not much of a mystery, though, because this figure, draped in luxurious purple cloth and covered in gold, sits on seven hills. That's our giveaway. Coins minted during the time of Vespasian show Rome as the goddess Roma, holding a sword pointed to the ground to symbolize an end to war—the Pax Romana—sitting on the seven hills of Rome. This was a significant image for the Roman Empire. John's figure looks like Rome, but has the name Babylon. However, this figure is not Rome or Babylon, or any particular city at all. She is the economic disparity that it takes to keep empire churning.[17]

When the seven bowls are at last exhausted and the final judgment is poured out, John says, "'Fallen! Fallen is Babylon the Great!' . . . For all the nations have drunk the maddening wine of her adulteries. The kings of the earth committed adultery with her, and the merchants of the earth grew rich from her excessive luxuries" (18:2–3). Everyone who trades ethics for profit is indicted here. But then he says this:

> The merchants of the earth will weep and mourn over her because no one buys their cargoes anymore—cargoes of gold, silver, precious stones and pearls; fine linen, purple, silk and scarlet cloth; every sort of citron wood, and articles of every kind made of ivory, costly wood, bronze, iron, and marble; cargoes of cinnamon and spice, of incense, myrrh and frankincense, of wine and olive oil, of fine flour and wheat; cattle and sheep; horses and carriages; and human beings sold as slaves. (18:11–13)

Everyone has been getting rich in this economy. Luxury and excess and illusions of royalty for everyone. So of course they are sad to see the good times end. But look closely at the merchandise John lists. In verse 13, he speaks of human beings sold as slaves or, more literally in the Greek, "human bodies." This is the Greek *soma*, or body. Enslaved people are not even slaves in this economy[18]—they are simply commodities to Rome.[19]

One of the best ways to illustrate this is with the tombstone of a Roman slave merchant named Aulus Caprillius

Timotheus.[20] We don't know much about Tim, but his grave marker is a chilling artifact. It's a carved stone with a triptych of images. The top panel shows Timotheus reclining on a couch served by some of his personal slaves. He is literally being fed grapes. Never let it be said that money can buy originality. Still, life was good for Tim!

The second panel shows another group of slaves. These people worked for him, farming his fields and gathering the grapes for his cup. Their work made his life comfortable. But in the bottom panel is a crowded mass of human bodies, chained together, being taken to the market to be sold. This is how Timotheus made his money. The trade of human bodies.

This is what John is saying the economy of the empire really looks like. Finely dressed in the most costly purple, seated peacefully on seven hills, yet drunk on the subjugation it takes to keep the economy churning. And all the while, our religion keeps us worshiping at the feet of what empire provides us, hiding from us the suffering down the ladder. John is trying to help us, perhaps force us, to see the hidden cost of our prosperity, to see just how deeply the economic tentacles of empire reach into our imagination. How often has the pursuit of a good deal led us to get in bed with injustice, preferring low cost over low impact or convenience over the treatment of employees? We can easily make stewardship an idol that prevents us from looking a few layers down to see the real impact of our purchases. This apocalyptic imagery isn't about monsters; it's about how monstrous our status quo can be.

However, before we reflect on this image, we need to address the gendered nature of this figure called Babylon. The luxurious cloth, the sexualized accusations, and the active role in enticing powerful men to their doom are all drawn from misogynist critiques of women prevalent in the Roman

Empire. Unfortunately, the writer of Revelation has fallen prey to something we often do, allowing one form of oppression to blind us to another. As Scholar Tina Pippen writes, "Power is deprivileged and eventually eliminated in the Apocalypse; whereas the ideology of gender is revalorized."[21] To be shaped properly by Revelation is not to stop where John stops. His imagination is contextualized by a specific time and place, after all. Instead, for Revelation to do its work, we must invite the vision to awaken us to all the ways that the principalities and powers around us work to keep us divided. Economic but also racial, gendered, and cultural barriers need to come down.

AN ECONOMIC PARABLE

In the gospels of Matthew and Luke, Jesus tells two versions of a fascinating parable. The version in Matthew is slightly more familiar, and is often called the parable of the talents (or bags of gold, in the NIV). In Luke, it is called the parable of the ten minas. What's interesting is that, in context, they seem to be saying opposite things.

In Matthew, a man travels and entrusts some of his wealth to his servants. One is given five talents, another two, and a final servant just one. The first two go and make a return on the money, whereas the third is more risk averse and saves the money in a hole until his boss gets home. Upon arriving home, the wealthy benefactor is excited to receive 100 percent return from these first two servants but is furious with the last one and casts him out into the dark (Matthew 25:30). Generally, we read this parable akin to the line from Spider-Man's uncle—With great responsibility comes great power. In other words, do your best with what you have to make sure God gets a return on investment on you. That's fine. There's some truth to that.

However, the parallel in Luke gives us a completely different spin on the same story. The narrative is essentially the same. But there are clues that we should be on our toes. Jesus says that a rich man went off to a distant land to make himself king. Perhaps in response to such arrogance, his subjects hated him and tried to spoil his coronation (Luke 19:12–14). If, indeed, this man is our stand-in for God in the story, it's already off to a rocky start. And perhaps because of that, the critique offered by the third servant rings even louder here in Luke. When the newly crowned king returns and asks for his money back, the third servant, the one who hid the money, says, "I was afraid of you, because you are a hard man. You take out what you did not put in and reap what you did not sow" (19:21). Strange description for the God character, no?

In Luke, the context for the story is particular. Jesus has traveled to a new city and met a man named Zacchaeus. He is a tax collector. He was hated by his neighbors, probably in part for collaborating with the Roman Empire but certainly for using his position to defraud them. Tax collectors were required to return a quota to Rome but often found ways to skim as much as they could from those assigned to them. In all, the role of a tax collector was to maximize the return to Rome.

Nevertheless, upon meeting Jesus, Zacchaeus declares that he has turned over a new leaf. He will give half of what he has to those in need and will work to repay everything he has stolen four times over (19:8). In response, Jesus addresses the crowd, which is already upset with him for giving attention to Zacchaeus, declaring that salvation has come to find this man. No one is beyond the reach of grace, and we should welcome a change of heart whenever it happens. But then we read, "While they were listening to this, he went on to tell them a parable" (19:11), and this is where Jesus unfolds the tale of the hated rich man and his dutiful servants.

It's quite a moment because you can imagine two things going on. First, a crowd that is skeptical about Zacchaeus's about-face. Does he really mean it? Will he follow through? And if he does, does that mean he gets off scot-free?

And then there's Zacchaeus. I take him at face value here—honest and hopefully wanting to make a change—but perhaps he had not quite thought through the implications.

And so Jesus addresses both audiences at once.

Zacchaeus works for Caesar. A hated king who took what he wanted regardless of the pain inflicted on those under his heel. A kingdom that the Jewish people had tried to sabotage and throw off repeatedly. One that welcomed collaborators but expected fealty at all costs, demanding a commitment to Roman objectives and discarding anyone under its wheel if necessary. And so Jesus says, Zacchaeus, I love your heart, but if you do this—if you return with only what Rome deserves, and you choose not to exploit every opportunity for growth, you will not be received well. You will undoubtedly be demoted; you may even be thrown out of your master's court, into the outer darkness. Are you sure you're ready for that?

In Luke, this parable is not a capitalist manifesto; it is a warning about the cost of doing what is right once you discover yourself ensnared by the beast. It's political power that lures us in, it's religion that convinces us to stay, but it's often economics that keeps us trapped.

THE CHALLENGE FOR US

In the first scene of this final cycle—the appearance of the red dragon—John tells us that evil is real and active in the world.

At the same time, he assures us that it has been defeated and overcome, utterly undone by the sacrifice of Christ. But now, lest we think we can sit back and wait for God to fix things, counting on the dragon to destroy itself, John challenges us to think about our response to evil.

The dragon is undone, evil is defeated, but politics, religion, and economics are the realms where we choose to support or challenge the world around us. In church we often talk about spiritual warfare. In John's imagination, the spiritual battle is over. It's done. Christ is victorious and has shown us that the way to victory is self-giving nonviolence. The spiritual battle that remains is the practical experience of living out that truth in real life.

And John does not pull his punches.

He says if your politics serves you and not your neighbor, it is evil. If your religion hides the violence of your voting record from you, it is evil. If you don't want to be marked with the beast, then push back against the oppression inherent in the economic systems surrounding you. And yes, he uses Rome as an example, but his target is something much bigger—the ways in which our principalities and powers can subtly come to dominate our vision of the world.

Today, Rome is long gone, the imperial cult has faded, and the world's economy has transitioned many times over since the first century. John's warnings, however, are as relevant as ever because he sees our vulnerability with incredible lucidity. The way that evil sneaks its way back into our story, disguising and transforming itself, again and again, to make us think that we can worship the Lamb without making hard choices.

The thing is, worship and transformation go hand in hand. And if the peace of Jesus doesn't bring us to increasingly peaceful politics, religion, and economics, then it has not landed properly in our hearts. And we are not prepared for the renewal of all things that God imagines.

10

GROUND ZERO

We've met the monsters. The beast from the sea—our love of political power. The beast from the land—our religion turned sideways. And the figure who rides the beast—our prosperity that has overtaken human flourishing. In all these monstrous examples, John lays bare the conspiracy that traps us—the resignation that there is no possibility greater than the status quo. It's not a malevolent Illuminati that controls the world; it is our collaboration with the systems that steal our prophetic imagination for what could be.

The irony is, we cling to our conspiracy theories. It's much easier to believe that the antichrist will appear and we will stand in a defiant show of heroic faith than it is to evaluate how our everyday voting and spending contribute to the injustice propped up by the religious services we attend.

Still, once these monsters have been unveiled as less threatening than we once imagined—pawns for a raging dragon who has already been defeated—we can now begin to imagine the expansiveness of Jesus' kingdom. That's what this chapter is about—Christ's defeat of evil and the welcome of the upside-down kingdom.

Let's start by going back to the beginning. When we first set out our guidelines for reading the Apocalypse, we looked at how the Hebrew prophets spoke in expanding concentric circles. We compared how Isaiah starts with the people of Israel, expanding to the nations surrounding his tribe, before pushing out to the furthest limits of his imagination, proclaiming the entire cosmos welcome into the story of renewal. This is the model that John has been using throughout Revelation. The same story of healing told three times with expanding scope and magnitude.

Like Isaiah, John begins by speaking to his people, the church. In the seven letters, he acknowledges that there are challenges as we follow the way of Jesus, but this is how the story ends:

> Here I am! I stand at the door and knock. If anyone hears my voice and opens the door, I will come in and eat with that person, and they with me.
>
> To the one who is victorious, I will give the right to sit with me on my throne, just as I was victorious and sat down with my Father on his throne. (Revelation 3:20–21)

In one sense, this is our salvation—the end of the story right here. A transformed life culminates as we sit at God's table. This is an image of that personal salvation we are familiar with. That, too, is very much part of John's imagination. But we're just getting started. Any conception of Christianity that ends with personal salvation is far from complete.

And so we start the story again. This time our attention is turned to the nations—God's plan for the redemption of the world. Through seals and trumpets our expectations are turned upside down as God reveals that grace will change the world. The sacrifice of the Lamb will open our eyes to the way we have scapegoated each other, trading peace for a cheap facsimile. This is how that story ends:

> We give thanks to you, Lord God Almighty,
>   the One who is and who was,
> because you have taken your great power
>   and have begun to reign.
> (Revelation 11:17)

This is no longer God who is to come; this is God arrived. The world is transformed through Christ. The nations are redeemed through the dismantling of our violence. The world's salvation is very much part of John's imagination as well. But we're not done yet.

THE REDEMPTION OF ALL THINGS

The story repeats one final time—this time with an eye to the defeat of evil and death. This time around, not just individuals, not just our world, but the entire cosmos will be healed by God. And this is the key to reading the seven bowls of wrath that are poured out in Revelation 16.

The seven seals unveil the contrast between the way of Jesus and the way of Domitian. Even as we reflect on what needs to crumble in order for real peace to arrive, the opening of the seventh seal introduces a pause before the story continues with the seven trumpets.

The seven trumpets show us the ineffectiveness of vengeance set against the power of nonviolent witness. We see that the grace of Jesus is better than our hopes for retribution, but evil still remains active in the world. The story begins again.

The seven bowls offer us a ringside seat to finally witness the end of all that threatens God's creation. And as we reach this final climax, we come to see the object of God's wrath limited to the examples of structural violence represented by monsters that threaten God's peace. But this is how the story, ultimately, ends:

> Then I saw "a new heaven and a new earth," for the first heaven and the first earth had passed away, and there was no longer any sea. I saw the Holy City, the new Jerusalem, coming down out of heaven from God, prepared as a bride beautifully dressed. (21:1–2)

The last time John described a city, it was the amalgam of Rome and Babylon—the economy as unfaithful partner to our politics. This city, the holy city, is a bride—everything our cities are not. It's even surrounded by imposing walls rendered useless by gates never shut (21:25). Everything about this final image is a subversion of what we might expect had we been the architects of salvation.

> God's dwelling place is now among the people, and he will dwell with them. They will be his people, and God himself will be with them and be their God. "He will wipe every tear from their eyes. There will be no more death" or mourning or crying or pain, for the old order of things has passed away. (21:3–4)

A worthy ending to our story, no doubt. God has promised to the rid the world of that which destroys, and indeed, nothing about this conclusion gives us warrant to imagine that God has renounced a significant portion of God's good creation. The climax here is transformation and healing, not abandonment. Still, there is a gap between the monsters that terrorize the world and this final, glorious expression of God's goodness. So how did we get to the end for the third (and final) time?

THE BATTLE OF ARMAGEDDON

Armageddon is a word that people seem to love. Surprisingly, it shows up only once in Revelation (Revelation 16:16). This presumed battle is part of the section that we refer to as the seven bowls. These are a retelling of a sort of the seven trumpets, which are a retelling of the seven seals, both of which we explored earlier. But if you can remember all the way back to the sixth trumpet, we read about a great army massing for a battle with God (9:13–19). However, that battle never happened. Instead, John was told not to write down what the voices of the seven thunders called for, and we were redirected to the witness of the Christ community that overcomes through nonviolence.

With the sixth bowl, we read about a similar scenario as all the kings of the earth prepare for a battle at a place called Armageddon. Armageddon is a compound of two Hebrew words, *har* and *Megiddo*. *Har* means mountain; Megiddo was a small town about sixty miles north of Jerusalem. Armageddon, as a word, simply means the mountain of Megiddo. But there are a couple of fascinating things here.

The first is that there is no such thing as the Mount of Megiddo.[1] In fact, there are only the plains of Megiddo, sometimes known as the valley of Jezreel.[2] There's not even a bump or a hill to be confused with a mountain. So clearly, as he's been doing all along, John is using this language figuratively to evoke an emotive response using "a mythical place-name."[3] It's almost as if he's saying, "I don't want anyone getting fixated on geography. Don't try to look for this on a map; we both know it doesn't exist anyway. Start thinking, searching for connections I might be suggesting with this language."

And once we do that, we find that Megiddo is an infamous location throughout the history of the Hebrews. In the fifteenth century BCE, possibly when the Hebrews were still enslaved, the Egyptian Thutmose III fought a massive battle against an alliance of Canaanite tribes led by the king of Kadesh. This battle doesn't appear in the Bible, because it's pre-Israelite history. Still, we do have some ancient records that describe it in detail.[4] Not so fun fact: This is the oldest known source of a body count. The battle was so huge that records indicate each army had over ten thousand troops massed for war.[5] When John describes a similar conflict with God, he says that there are not twice ten thousand troops at that battle but twice ten thousand *times* ten thousand, as if to suggest that the Battle of Megiddo was nothing compared to this conflict.

In 609 BCE, there was another great battle at Megiddo. This time, the Egyptian king Necho II and the Assyrians went to war against the Babylonians. The Hebrews, unfortunately, ended up being caught in the middle. Egypt came and said to Israel, "Can we pass through your land on our way to fight with the Babylonians?" But when Necho passed through, King Josiah traveled to meet him, and the pharaoh killed him at Megiddo (2 Kings 23:29). The Hebrews were betrayed and pulled into the battle, which eventually led to their downfall, as Judah was conquered by Babylon after Babylon defeated Assyria and Egypt. The Hebrew people were taken into exile, adding to the bad memories of Megiddo.

That's not all, though, because the judge Deborah and her military leader Barak battled the Canaanites at Megiddo (Judges 4:6–16; 5:19). Gideon went to war with the Midianites at Megiddo (Judges 7). King Saul was defeated by the Philistines on the plains of Megiddo (1 Samuel 29:1; 31:1–7). And the ancient historian Eusebius even records that the Romans set up a permanent camp at Megiddo known as "Legio in the great plain."[6] There were at least seven major historical conflicts at Megiddo that John would have been aware of.[7] However, the most crucial reference might be Zechariah, who links God's fight against the enemies of Israel to the mourning of Megiddo (Zechariah 12:9; 12:11).

The bottom line is that Megiddo conjures all kinds of war imagery, and now John tells us that evil meets God face-to-face at the mythic mountain of Megiddo. This is not a physical location; it's a very ancient way of saying that evil will meet its ground zero.

What happens in your head when I say it that way? Do you think of the Twin Towers and September 11? Of course you do. But you don't imagine that I am talking literally about a plot of land in New York City. We understand the emotion and significance of the moment evoked by the literary choice. That's what John is doing here. He's pulling from the history of Israel to evoke an emotion; he's describing not a place, but a feeling.

THE RIDER ON THE WHITE HORSE

If this battle doesn't happen at a physical location, how should we picture it? John helps us with that as well. We read: "I saw heaven standing open and there before me was a white horse, whose rider is called Faithful and True. With justice he judges and wages war. . . . He is dressed in a robe dipped in blood, and his name is the Word of God" (Revelation 19:11, 13).

This is Jesus. And here he is wielding a sword, covered in blood. Have we finally reached the violent confrontation we have waited for from page one—the Rambo-Jesus who will crush all opposition?

In a word, no. Because John turns our expectations upside down once again.

First, "justice" here is the word *dikaiosune* in Greek. However, in Hebrew and in Greek, this is the same word as "righteousness." It's actually an interesting quirk of the English language that we separate doing what is right religiously or spiritually from doing what is right in the world. This bifurcation doesn't exist in the biblical imagination. Nor does it exist in most other languages. So yes, this rider wages war, but no, it's not with weapons. It is with righteousness.

Next, his robe is dipped in blood even before the battle starts. Violence is revealed in the story once again—Revelation has no problem naming the world's violence—but this violence has occurred earlier in the story. The rider's robe is bloody, but this is not an enemy's blood; this is the evidence of Christ's own sacrifice.

Finally, John tells us that out of the rider's mouth comes a sharp sword to strike down the nations (19:15). Contrary to our popular imagination, this rider does not have a sword in his hand at all. He wields a sword, but it comes from his mouth. As we have seen repeatedly in Revelation, victory is won not with weapons, war, or force but through the testimony of nonviolence (12:11).

You have to almost willfully reject the biblical witness to imagine this sword being any kind of physical weapon. The writer of Hebrews describes the words of Scripture being sharper than any double-edged sword (Hebrews 4:12). Isaiah, on whom John is relying heavily for the imagery, says that the suffering servant's mouth will be like a sharpened sword (Isaiah 49:2; cf. Psalms 59:7; 64:3). Even the apostle Paul transposes the imagery of a sword for nonviolent purposes (Ephesians 6:17). In fact, all the way back in the opening cycle of Revelation, Jesus already declared that he would overcome evil with the sword of his mouth (Revelation 2:16). Any interpretation that even hints at Jesus using a weapon to kill is a complete misreading.

But there's more.

Because not only is John turning our expectations upside down—he is also subverting even the prophetic imagination of justice.

This image of the rider on the white horse is lifted directly from Isaiah. The prophet describes the day of God's vengeance, a day Jesus intentionally leaves out of his mandate when he quotes him (Isaiah 61:2; Luke 4:19). But when Isaiah describes that fateful day, we see a similar mysterious figure.

> Who is this coming from Edom,
>   from Bozrah, with his garments stained crimson?
> Who is this, robed in splendor,
>   striding forward in the greatness of his strength?
>
> "It is I, proclaiming victory,
>   mighty to save."
>
> Why are your garments red,
>   like those of one treading the winepress?
>
> "I have trodden the winepress alone;
>   from the nations no one was with me.
> I trampled them in my anger
>   and trod them down in my wrath;
> their blood spattered my garments,
>   and I stained all my clothing."
> (Isaiah 63:1–3)

Isaiah describes what we have been led to expect from a lifetime of envisioning God through the lens of human blood and war—a God who enacts justice the way we might. But as we saw in the throne room, the lion we expected has been exchanged for something surprising—the Lamb of peace. No longer are we limited to interpreting human words about God, now the very Word of God walks with us. And it is this

Jesus who appears with only his testimony of nonviolence to save the day. In this moment, Jesus is both the culmination of our longing and the overturning of everything we thought to hope for.[8]

The pernicious idea that Jesus will come back someday, riding on a horse, galloping through town and lopping off heads, is a blatant misreading of what is going on here. It contradicts both the Lamb revealed in Revelation and the Jesus we encounter in the Gospels, and it completely misses what John is trying to do—turn our expectation of justice upside down. The painful irony is that for a book that never mentions an antichrist, misreadings of this image that diminish the nonviolence of Jesus are anti-Christ.

Armageddon is not a geographic location to find on a map. The sword is not a physical weapon Jesus wields. The blood on his garment is a picture of sacrifice, not war. This is an image of the power of the cross to overcome evil, dismantle violence, upend terror, and put right the world.

But if you're not yet convinced, look at what happens when Jesus arrives. There's not much of a battle.

The beast and the kings of the earth and their armies gather for war. The tension ratchets up. But without so much as a single shot, the first beast and the false prophet (this is a reference to the second beast from Revelation 13:11–17) are captured and thrown into the fire. Those who stand with evil are killed with the sword from the rider's mouth, and the birds gorge themselves on their flesh (19:19–21).

Granted, this is pretty dark and a little bit gruesome. There's no point in denying that. John does not want us to miss for a second the gravity of what he's talking about here. Still, in the larger context of this letter and the way John has been using these images, this is clearly not meant to be a battle that you could place on a map or compile a body count from. This is an image of how the story of Christ disarms the destroyers of the earth (11:18).

Yes, the beast and the prophet—the power of political empire and the witness of false religion—are thrown into the fire to be destroyed. But this climactic image of judgment is reserved for abstract representations of evil,[9] not its victims. Even those kings of the earth, killed by Jesus' sword, are later welcomed into the new Jerusalem to find healing once the city descends (21:24; 22:2).[10] All of this is an image of the power of Christ's sacrifice that puts to death the way of sin in us (Romans 6:6; 1 Peter 2:24).

As scholar Loren Johns describes, "Central to the Lamb Christology of the Apocalypse is the forging of a new understanding of the means by which one conquers: that of a consistent, nonviolent resistance born of clear allegiance to God."[11] And this arrival of Jesus here at the climax of the story is the height of John's subversive imagination. All our hopes are met, undermined, and elevated. And we should have seen it all coming.

MUSTARD SEED

There are two significant images left to explore in Revelation—the millennial reign and the city of the new Jerusalem. Before we continue, though, there is a particular parable of Jesus that serves as a useful metaphor for John's movement here from victory to consummation. In Revelation we see that Jesus triumphs over evil by subverting our imagination of victory, replacing our need for violence with expansive welcome. And we see how small seeds of new possibility take root in the hearts of individuals, who become communities, who reshape politics, which leads to the reordering of the cosmos.

These two ideas, the inversion of our expectations and the power of small things to change the world, come together beautifully in Matthew 13. Jesus tells the story of a mustard seed. It's one of his most famous parables and has become part of our popular consciousness at this point. However, a layer to the story is sometimes lost on us.

> The kingdom of heaven is like a mustard seed, which a man took and planted in his field. Though it is the smallest of all seeds, yet when it grows, it is the largest of garden plants and becomes a tree, so that the birds come and perch in its branches. (13:31–32)

Small things grow in unexpected ways. Simple yet profound. But to leave it at that is to miss the apocalyptic nature of Jesus' parable.

The first clue of something disruptive is the ill-suited description of a mustard bush, which according to Jesus, grows into a large garden plant and becomes a tree. Now, it's true that mustard seeds are tiny. Around the time of Jesus, they were used proverbially as an illustration in this way.[12] And they did grow into large and unruly plants. Extensive rules specifically addressed how mustard bushes tended to creep across manicured garden lines in contravention of Levitical rules about the mixing of seeds (Leviticus 19:19).[13] They were not, however, by any reasonable stretch, trees. Truthfully, they were more like scrubby, scraggly thickets. Not particularly regal. This is not a mistake, though. Jesus is up to something.

Unfortunately, part of the reference is obscured for us in English translations. If we return to the original language, what we read in Matthew 13:32 is that the mustard seed becomes a tree so that the birds of the air come and perch in its branches. That reference to the birds "of the air" is not superfluous; it's a callback. In fact, everything after "the largest of garden plants" is a scriptural reference.

In the Hebrew Scriptures, Israel is referred to using these words. The prophets imagine Israel becoming a place of refuge for the nations when God's kingdom arrives.

> This is what I saw;
>> there was a tree at the center of the earth,
>> and its height was great.
> The tree grew great and strong,
>> its top reached to heaven,
>> and it was visible to the ends of the whole earth.
> Its foliage was beautiful,
>> its fruit abundant,
>> and it provided food for all.
> The animals of the field found shade under it,
>> the birds of the air nested in its branches,
>> and from it all living beings were fed.
> (Daniel 4:10–12 NRSV)

Here's another example:

> This is what the Sovereign LORD says: I myself will take a shoot from the very top of a cedar and plant it; I will break off a tender sprig from its topmost shoots and plant it on a high and lofty mountain. . . . It will produce branches and bear fruit and become a splendid cedar. Birds of every kind will nest in it; they will find shelter in the shade of its branches. (Ezekiel 17:22–23)

Note the imagery here. Something small, in this example a tiny, tender sprig, becomes an enormous cedar and provides shelter for the birds, which represent the nations. Familiar, right?

These are beautiful images of God's kingdom that were embedded in the Jewish consciousness, ideas that over time shaped their hope for what the world could become. The details that Jesus recounts—something small that becomes a great tree providing shelter and safety for the birds of the air—are not redundant; they are callbacks to the prophetic imagination of Jesus' people. Except, what does Jesus do with that memory? He both affirms and subverts it.

Just as John takes Isaiah's image of the divine warrior and reimagines it as the God who comes to save through self-sacrifice, so Jesus takes the image of kingdom that has become entangled with national pride and flips it upside down.

God's kingdom is remarkable. And it does start small. And it will grow unstoppable. And if you choose to be part of it, it will be glorious. But it will not look the way you expect it to, because the kingdom is less a majestic cedar—strong and imposing—and more a scruffy mustard bush notorious for creeping across boundaries and showing up where you don't want it. It's a pretty remarkable moment akin to taking America's symbolic eagle and replacing it with a seagull. Or perhaps swapping Isaiah's divine warrior with the image of a slain lamb.

Philosopher Slavoj Žižek loves to tell the story of caffeine-free Diet Coke.[14] Once upon a time, there was a drink called Coca-Cola. It was made with sugar and caffeine and cocaine and sold as a tonic for "most ailments." It tasted awful, but it had a certain obvious appeal, likely because of the cocaine. Eventually, we realized that cocaine was not healthy, and it was removed. Then we realized that massive amounts of sugar were also bad for us, and that too was replaced. Later, we began to consider our caffeine intake, and caffeine was removed as well. Today, people spend millions of dollars drinking a soda that has nothing to do with the product that started it all.

Now, if you enjoy caffeine-free Diet Coke, by all means, continue. The point Žižek makes is that we have a way of emptying things of everything but the name so that they can become whatever we want them to be. The prophets spoke of God's kingdom as refuge for all, a living, growing, thriving thing that welcomes all, providing safety and nourishment irrespective of what comes. That feels very much like the God at work throughout the Hebrew story.

Yet slowly over time, that image of motherly nurture became one of muscular strength. Warriors and walls replaced refuge and welcome in our imagination. An open-door kingdom somehow became hemmed in by garden lines, as horticulturists built scarecrows to shoo away the birds. A decidedly domesticated vision when held up against God's wild abandon. And so, with a simple parable, Jesus turns our imagination upside down in ways that reveal both God's intent and the smallness of our boundary keeping.

God is out there building God's kingdom, and we can participate in it through the smallest choices, says Jesus. Faith like a mustard seed and all that. But the real beauty of what grows from our belief is when we become the kind of people with the courage to cross our manicured boundaries to welcome those we once tried to scare away. When that happens, new communities form and new politics take shape, and slowly, inevitably, the world is transformed.

In other words, Jesus offers us a parable we already know, but twisted just enough to draw us back to the beauty we've lost sight of. That's precisely what John does here in Revelation. God is on our side. God will come to fight for us. Of course God will. God is good. That story could not be more true. But God will do so not by destroying our enemies, but by dismantling our idea of an enemy and teaching us to welcome even those we tried to push away.

The salvation of God is so much better than we had imagined.

THE MILLENNIUM

Political power and false religion are thrown into the fiery lake (Revelation 19:20). The dragon himself is locked away. And Christ reigns on the earth for a thousand years (20:2).

But then the dragon is set free! He gathers another army and tries for a second Armageddon. Specifically, we get an obscure reference to the nations of Gog and Magog from the corners of the earth. The only other biblical reference to these names comes from Ezekiel. There Gog, from the land of Magog, seems to be an archetypal enemy representative of any force that opposes God (Ezekiel 38:2). That lines up with an extra-biblical reference from 4 Ezra, which speaks of Gog and Magog as "gathered from the four winds of heaven" (4 Ezra 13:5). It looks like John is combining these references to talk about "the resilience of evil."[15] And that's a theme we've seen before in Revelation—recall the beast that could have a head chopped off and still find a way to hold on to power.

Regardless, the mutiny doesn't get far, as fire falls from heaven, devouring the armies, and this time evil is destroyed (Revelation 20:9–10). After that, those who had died are raised, and death and Hades are cast into the fire as well (20:14). Remember what we read at the start of this cycle; now comes the time to destroy that which destroys the earth (11:18). This is not the earth gone up in a puff of smoke; this is the God who heals all of creation from what ails it.

But what about this millennial reign? Even though John dedicates a total of two verses to it, this thousand-year period has been at the center of all kinds of speculation for a very long time.

These verses can be approached in several ways. *Millenarianism* is a blanket term for several literal interpretations of these verses. The common thread is a belief that there will be an actual historical thousand-year reign on earth. And while perhaps less common, it was certainly present in the hopes of the earliest Christian communities. Papias, Justin Martyr, and Irenaeus all expressed support for some form of this view.[16]

When the Reformers came along in the fifteenth century, they developed a form of millenarianism called postmillennialism. This view imagined Christ returning only after a literal millennial reign *of the church*. They believed that Christ would return once the church had prepared the way for him. Men like John Calvin and Ulrich Zwingli took to setting up Christian city-states, thinking that Christ would come and take his rightful place if they could create a just world. The irony, is that this top-down imposition of righteousness ended up looking a lot like the terror imposed by the very empire John mocks in Revelation.[17]

Regardless, this profound hope in humanity's ability to institute a righteous worldwide reign came crashing down in the First and Second World Wars. As our optimism about humanity's peaceful capacity began to wane, another millenarian view came into vogue. This one we call premillennialism. This approach once again imagines a literal thousand-year reign but sees the world getting worse and worse, waiting for the time when Christ will finally show up and establish his kingdom. Rather than using *our* power to force a Christian reign, this theory hopes for a more muscular Jesus in the vein of the divine warrior that John undermines.

However, we have already observed how deeply John incorporates apocalyptic imagery into his writing. His goal has consistently been to turn those expectations upside down, but it's clear he is aware of the popular tropes. And this concept of a temporary paradise on earth is a familiar one in the apocalyptic genre.

An Ethiopic apocalypse called 1 Enoch imagines a time of testing after which a government of the righteous will reign during an eighth week of creation.[18] A Syriac apocalypse called 2 Baruch describes a time of incredible blessing followed by the glorious return of the Messiah.[19] Likewise, 4 Ezra narrates the story of a restored Jerusalem and "an earthly paradise for the righteous."[20] Finally, the *Apocalypse of Elijah* explicitly mentions a thousand-year reign of the righteous.[21]

To imagine that John continually borrows imagery from his apocalyptic counterparts specifically to subvert them to only now treat them as gospel feels like running off course right before the finish line.

This is perhaps why allegorical interpretations of the millennial reign were prevalent in the earliest years of Christianity. For example, Oecumenius, who wrote the first Greek commentary on Revelation, described a literal millennial reign as Greek atheistic nonsense.[22] However, it was probably Augustine who popularized the major alternative we sometimes call amillennialism.[23] Amillennialism means "no millennium," but that's a bit of a misnomer. This view doesn't say there is no millennium so much as it says that the millennium is a metaphor for the reign of Christ in the church. While postmillennialists imagine the church preparing the way for Christ's reign, amillennialists recognize the seeds of the kingdom as already sown, the roots inevitably working their way throughout the world. What we are waiting for is not the victory of Christ; that already happened on the cross when the power of sin was broken. What we wait for now is the slow creeping growth of a mustard bush–like kingdom that crosses boundaries, shows up where we least expect, and continues to welcome in those we once pushed away. Christ already reigns (Revelation 11:17); it's we who need to catch up.

THE LAKE OF FIRE

What then of the lake of fire? So far, the scariest images in Revelation have been reserved for the conceptual images of evil. Deception and power and death and Hades, all those anti-god forces, are explicitly thrown into the fire just as we were promised at the start of this cycle (Revelation 11:18). But just before we reach this final image of a renewed world, we read one final horror.

> Anyone whose name was not found written in the book of life was thrown into the lake of fire. (20:15)

And that should give any peaceful interpretation pause.

Certainly, we can acknowledge that we are so far into the realm of metaphor and hyperbole here that any attempt to build a definitive understanding of these words is fraught with subjectivity. However, a close reading of the words John chooses and a comparison to one more parable of Jesus can be helpful. The thing is, the English translators are doing a lot of work on our behalf, and some of it is perhaps not particularly helpful. For example, the phrase "anyone whose name" appears nowhere in the Greek text of Revelation 20:15. To take the verse word for word, we read something like:

> and | if | a certain one | not |found | in | the | book | of life | written | thrown | into | the | lake | of fire.

Now the thrust is pretty clear. Anything not written in God's book of life is destined for destruction. We already knew that was coming (see 11:18). What's not entirely clear is what this singular Greek pronoun *tis*, or "a certain one," refers to.[24] Granted, it's usually a someone, but it can also be a something.

Jesus tells a similar story in Matthew 13. Interestingly, it comes right after his story about the mustard seed. This time it's about how the kingdom of God is like a net dragged through the water, catching all kinds. Translations often say "all kinds of fish," but Jesus leaves it at "all kinds." And that makes some sense. Jesus specifically says this is a dragnet.[25] The type of net that has weights on one side so it can be dragged along the floor, stirring up fish or crabs and seaweed, maybe lost sandals even, catching all of it in the net to be dragged onto shore for sorting. And that's what happens in the story. The net is pulled up on the beach, and the catch is sorted out from everything else in the net. The good goes in the basket. The bad is set aside. Again, no fish are mentioned here. God's kingdom, it seems, sweeps through the world, gathering up everything to be sorted.

And Jesus says this is an image of how it will be in the end. "The angels will come and separate the wicked from the righteous and throw them into the blazing furnace, where there will be weeping and gnashing of teeth" (Matthew 13:49–50). Again, we have an image of fire and wickedness thrown into it. But once again, we have personalized it in unhelpful ways. The dragnet in the original parable catches more than fish; it gathers up everything to be sorted. In the parallel Jesus gives us, the righteous are separated from the wicked, but once again, we come against a somewhat flexible pronoun. This time it's the Greek word *autos*, or the third-person plural "them." That tends to immediately make us think of persons, but the pronoun can equally refer to a plural group of things.[26] Things like the flotsam inevitably caught in the type of net Jesus describes.

For Jesus, the kingdom sweeps through the world, gathering up everything it touches, dragging it all onto the beach to be sorted, where everything righteous will be saved, and all that is wicked will be burned away.[27] That sounds surprisingly faithful to what John describes here in Revelation. Any *thing* not found in the book of life will be thrown into the fire along with all deception and lies and deceit, with the death and sin and violence that destroys God's creation.

That's a sobering thought to imagine, to be sure. When I am finally scooped up and dragged to God's beach, there are assuredly some things that will come with me that will need to burn away. Maybe it's the selfishness that lives inside me or the chronic pain you suffer with. It's undoubtedly the systems that keep people from flourishing and the insurmountable debts that we have accumulated. But one day, all of that, everything that pushes back against the goodness of God and destroys God's creation, will need to be sorted and discarded. As difficult as it is for me to imagine that someone could intentionally reject all that is good in the universe forever, what I hear John saying is that everything within me that rejects the divine will one day meet its end. And yet God will never give up on any of us.

As the church father Origin writes, "Blessed, then, is the one who is baptized in the Holy Spirit and does not need the baptism by fire, but three times unhappy is that person who has need to be baptized in fire, though Jesus takes care of both of them."[28]

11

THE NEW CITY

Evil has met its Megiddo. Christ has assumed his rightful place in the world. Finally, John sees the new Jerusalem, an image of heaven, as his vision comes to a close. "Then I saw 'a new heaven and a new earth,' for the first heaven and the first earth had passed away, and there was no longer any sea" (Revelation 21:1).

The concept of heaven is inherently in the realm of speculative fiction. We are talking about an experience never tasted by a human we can speak to. Using language drawn from this life to talk about a next life is always going to be incomplete. Perhaps knowing that, John employs language to signal that we need to stay in an imaginative space as we contemplate. The phrase a "new heaven and a new earth" has been pulled directly from the prophet Isaiah (Isaiah 65:17), but the counterpart of the old heaven and earth "passing away" comes from the apocalyptic vision of 1 Enoch.[1] Once again, John is juxtaposing different eschatological visions.

And that's important to reference because the intent is actually renewal rather than replacement. Misinterpretations of this passing-away motif have led Christians to assume that the world will one day be discarded. That has led some to reject climate science, believing global climate change is an inevitable part of some divine plan to replace the earth. It's contributed to dominion replacing stewardship in our imagination of creation care, assuming the earth to be a temporary home.

On the contrary, though, 1 Enoch, which John quotes, clarifies that this "passing away" is not a trashing at all but instead a promise to "transform the earth and make it a blessing."[2] That's much more in line with what we already know about how this story ends—the destruction of that which destroys and the vow to make all things new (Revelation 11:18; 21:5). With that in mind, we shouldn't be too thrown off when the fiery lake makes one final appearance.

> The cowardly, the unbelieving, the vile, the murderers, the sexually immoral, those who practice magic arts, the idolaters and all liars—they will be consigned to the fiery lake of burning sulfur. (21:8)

Keep in mind that the old has passed away at this point in the story. Evil, death, and Hades are already done away with. It seems that in the narrative of the Apocalypse, this final appearance of the fire is one ultimate farewell to all that has been corrupted by sin in God's creation. I don't think it's a stretch to hope that this verse describes not a torment for souls, but instead a destination for all the broken identities that can, at last, be discarded now that God dwells among us (21:3).

In fact, it must be that, because after this consignment, we are told that the gates of heaven will never shut (21:25) and that those who hold on to these corrupted identities remain outside the city (22:15) until they are ready to enter. The fiery lake of heaven is that which burns away whatever we need to let go of in order to enter. And that feels very much in line with the language used throughout the New Testament.

In one particularly aggressive passage, Paul writes that "the wrath of God is being revealed from heaven against all the godlessness and wickedness of people" (Romans 1:18). But hewing precisely to what Paul says, without adding anything to it, reveals a striking similarity to what we see here in John's image of heaven. For Paul, God's anger is constrained to our wickedness, with divine wrath focused on all the spaces where we are unlike the peace of God.

In Revelation, that same wrath, imagined as a fiery lake, is reserved for all that hurts us and destroys God's creative investment. God is love. Therefore, God's actions, acts of anger included, can only ever be an expression of that love. For wrath to be loving, it must be the destruction of those anti-god forces that destroy, which means it must also be grace for God's children. Even our perception of divine anger is turned upside down in the end.

THE NEW JERUSALEM

And now we see the city itself. Enormous walls with gates named for the twelve tribes of Israel (Revelation 21:12). Foundations named for the twelve apostles of the church (21:14). This city is the culmination of both the Jewish and the Christian stories—everything points to this summit. Heaven itself is another reminder that supersessionist ideas of the church replacing the Jewish people are not only problematic but also deeply out of step with the biblical imagination. The story only ever expands, never cutting people out.

Still, heaven itself is less a destination and more a final transformation of our hopes.

The city is a perfect cube, and conspicuously fifteen hundred miles long and wide and tall (21:16).[3] That shape would have immediately conjured memories of the inner sanctuary of the Jewish temple, itself a perfect cube of twenty cubits on each side (1 Kings 6:20). However, the even more striking comparison might be to Ezekiel, which also describes a renewed Jerusalem. In Ezekiel's vision, the city is a square city measuring 4,500 cubits, or roughly one and a half miles per side (Ezekiel 48:15–16). The heavenly city is a thousand times bigger and somehow also a dimension greater, going fifteen hundred miles straight up. An ancient structure towering fifteen hundred miles into the sky was inconceivable, and this is undoubtedly intentional. Heaven defies our imagination.

Famously, the footings of the walls are made with precious stones, and the streets are made of gold (Revelation 21:19–21). We read this and often imagine the opulence of heaven, but to my mind, the vision offers a last subtle critique of wealth. Rather than the extravagance associated with the economy of Rome, the city of heaven suggests that everything we have given inordinate value will one day be as insignificant as asphalt. The jewelry and gold we have worked so hard to acquire, now buried underground and trod underfoot. Heaven is an indictment of our fascination with wealth, not a celebration of it. Just one more way our expectations are flipped.

John also enumerates the twelve layers of precious stone related to the twelve foundations of the city and embedded in the four walls. The specific gems seem to be related to those arranged in four rows on the breastplate of the Hebrew high priest (Exodus 28:17–20).[4] Suspiciously, these are also the twelve stones associated with the zodiac. The zodiac has roots that extend well back into human antiquity, but it also featured prominently in astrology that the Romans adopted from the Greeks. John seems to make this secondary reference explicit by listing the stones in their zodiacal order, moving counterclockwise around the circle like the zodiacal sun.[5] Except he embeds the stones in the foundations of the four walls, evoking the rows from the breastplate again. John seems to intentionally mix the two reference points, combining the arrangement from Exodus with the order from the zodiac, perhaps to ensure that diverse audiences see themselves reflected in heaven.[6] We are drawn from every tribe and tongue and nation, and, it would seem, we bring our stories with us (Revelation 7:9).

However, probably the most striking feature of this city is that there is no temple (21:22). There is no need for it. There are no sacrifices, no priests, no disconnect between God and people to be rectified; we are finally one. There is no pursuit of scapegoats or religious violence—no need to drive anyone away to justify ourselves ever again. Christ has dismantled our desire to see a scapegoat excluded in order to know we are loved. In fact, the gates of heaven never shut (21:25), because the need to know that someone else has been left outside has been completely abandoned.

Still, outside the gates remain those who refuse to come in—those who hold on to their identities shaped in mistrust and fear (22:15). The angel says to John, "Let the one who does wrong continue to do wrong; let the vile person continue to be vile; let the one who does right continue to do right; and let the holy person continue to be holy" (22:11). In heaven, our commitment to the good no longer depends on the expectation of someone else being punished. It's a small moment, but it's also one of my favorites in Revelation. In the fullness of heaven, we are freed not only from our sins, but also from the insatiable desire to compare and compete, to define our value through the exclusion of another. And that itself might be the heart of salvation—to embrace the way of peace for its own sake, trusting that there is no end to second chances.

We are told that all the nations will come to the city (21:26). Heaven is an expansive and abounding image of grace that extends beyond our ethnocentric tendencies. In fact, the city even has a river that flows out from the center and fruit trees that never go out of season (22:1–2), a constant gift even for those who reject its invitation. This image is specific, though, because in ancient cities, people, often conscripted laborers, worked for years to build massive aqueducts that would bring water inside the walls. And Rome spent a fortune building roads that enabled food to be transported to the city. Yet these public infrastructure projects that were the pride of the empire are entirely unnecessary in an abundance economy that gives away rather than hoards for itself. Think back to John's warning to the church in Laodicea.

And still, in heaven, we work and harvest; we come and go. This is not a disembodied spiritual realm that John is imagining. This is the world healed. There is no "flying away to glory," only God come to fix, redeem, save, transform, renew, and reimagine creation.

So when, finally, the One on the throne speaks, and says, "Behold, I am making all things new" (21:5 ESV), we witness the full expansion of the prophetic imagination. Where Isaiah could only muster the courage to imagine God doing a new thing (Isaiah 43:19), John sees all things transformed.

The apocalypse is not the destruction of the earth. It's not the end of the world. It is the renewal of everything God touches. Everyone, everything, every system, every imagination, every expression of God's creative good, healed and set right. The voice of the Amen says, "Here I am! I stand at the door and knock. If anyone hears my voice and opens the door, I will come in and eat with that person, and they with me" (Revelation 3:14, 20). This humble dinner invitation will change the world. That's the upside-down apocalypse.

Revelation is the culmination of the prophetic hope that runs from Genesis and the rest of the Torah into the Prophets and through the Christian Scriptures, embodied on the cross and now manifest in creation. The world cannot be doomed, it is made by God. And the future belongs to those individuals and communities and systems and nations that move ahead of the curve, trusting that all creation evolves to live in harmony with God's good pleasure.

For me, this is part of the underrated beauty of Revelation. It reminds us that as hard as the work is, our efforts to transform the world are not wasted. They are part of an inevitable kingdom started by Jesus that is slowly seeding the world with peace. It's easy to get overwhelmed by the injustice that surrounds us. In fact, the more aware we become of the types of despotism that Revelation unveils, the easier it is to slip into a posture of apocalyptic pessimism. But if we stick with it and follow the story through, what we discover is that our actions for peace, for justice and equity, for inclusion and diversity, are not naive hopes in a fractured world. They are the stuff of destiny.

AN OLD STORY

An old saying attributed to Zen teacher Qingyuan Weixin says, "At the first, he saw mountains as mountains and rivers as rivers. Then he saw that mountains are not mountains and rivers are not rivers. Until finally, he saw once again that mountains were mountains and rivers were rivers."[7]

This has been my experience of Revelation.

At first, the river was a river, and the mountain was a mountain. I had clear ideas about this book, an imagination of the apocalypse that had been formed by speculation and conspiracy, stamped by childish fears that I would be left behind. In truth, my assumptions were based as much on respectability politics and commonsense economics as on theological pretense. I assumed God was as fearful and vengeful as I can be, and so I read accordingly.

Yet as I worked my way through the text, I began to discover that the river was no longer a river, and the mountain was no longer a mountain. I was surprised to discover that terms like *antichrist* and *rapture* never appear anywhere in the text. It was disconcerting to see that images from Greek mythology and the Roman imperial cult had found their way into my Bible. And as I saw those images presented in a new light, I found that my longing for the strength of a lion was slowly being replaced with a fascination for the peaceful way of the Lamb.

However, as I stuck with the journey and continued to learn, I gradually returned to trusting that the river was a river, and the mountain was indeed a mountain. The sovereignty of God was different than I had expected. Less anxious and more confident. Motivated by self-assured repair rather than furious despair. This was a trustworthy vision. One that I had to work hard to understand but one that has brought me back to the Gospels and the peace of Christ in which I have grounded my faith.

Revelation is not a map of history, but neither is it an apocalypse in the sense we often imagine. It is, in fact, a profound statement about the goodness of God and the unfolding of time, and a reminder that nothing is left to chance. The upside-down apocalypse is prophetic proclamation that God's love undoubtedly wins—and the profound trust that the Spirit is active and present, pulling history back toward the Creator.

So let me finish with this affirmation. The river is a river, and the mountain is a mountain. God is on the throne, and Jesus is the foundation for our faith and our model for peaceful action in the world.

Amen.

ACKNOWLEDGMENTS

I've said it before, but it bears repeating, I want to acknowledge my partner Rachel Duncan for all the support and encouragement over now twenty-one years of marriage and however long it took to research and write this book. Thank you.

In addition, I'd like to acknowledge:

The community of Commons Church, in particular Janice Hsu-Chan, who served as the board chair during the time I was writing and has always championed all of our pastoral team to explore our voices in new and interesting ways.

My professor, Dr. Beth Stovell, who guided my research at Ambrose University and Seminary and created the space for me to carefully refine my ideas.

Laura Thiessen, who provided a first read of my initial jumble of thoughts and helped me find the thread through it all. This book is better for your notes.

My friends, Joe Manafo and Bobbi Salkeld, who have pushed me to think more broadly and read more widely and whose lives have always affirmed my faith even when I'm not sure of it.

And finally, Jesus, who continues to inspire and challenge me to uncover the peaceful path you laid. My theology continues to evolve but you remain the center of it.

NOTES

PREFACE

1. Read Du Mez, *Jesus and John Wayne*.

CHAPTER 1

1. LaHaye and Jenkins, *Left Behind*.
2. Danker, Bauer, Arndt, and Gingrich (hereafter BDAG), *Greek-English Lexicon*, 112. Cf. Romans 16:25; Ephesians 3:3.
3. This idea was perhaps best formulated by Karl Rahner in what is often called Rahner's Rule: "The 'economic' Trinity is the 'immanent' Trinity, and the 'immanent' Trinity is the 'economic' Trinity." Rahner, *The Trinity*, 22.
4. Tobin, "*Logos*," in Freedman, *Anchor Yale Bible Dictionary* (hereafter *AYBD*), 4:347.
5. "*Logos* was associated with discourse or rational explanation." Tobin.
6. Tobin.
7. Silva, ed., *Dictionary New Testament Theology*, 3:132.

CHAPTER 2

1. Brueggemann, *Interpretation and Obedience*, 185. I also love this quote from the same book that I think captures John's mission well: "The key pathology of our time, which seduces us all, is the reduction of imagination so that we are too numbed, satiated, and co-opted to do serious imaginative work" (199).

2. "In Judaism apocalypticism is the 'successor' of prophecy." Schüssler Fiorenza, *Book of Revelation*, 169.

3. Koester, *Revelation*, 72.

4. Tacitus, *Historae* 2.8.

5. Irenaeus, *Adversus haereses* 5.30.3.

6. Eusebius, *Historia ecclesiastica* 3.20.8–9.

7. Koester, *Revelation*, 76; Caird, *Revelation of St. John*, 7; Yarbro Collins, *Crisis and Catharsis*, 55; Mounce, *Book of Revelation*, 21.

8. Suetonius, *Domitianus* 8.1–12.3.

9. Koester, *Revelation*, 77.

10. Koester, 96.

11. Linton, "Reading the Apocalypse," in Barr, *Reality of Apocalypse*, 9.

12. Kent, *Interpretation and Genre*, 151.

13. Linton, "Reading the Apocalypse," 22.

14. Linton, 33; Koch, *Rediscovery of Apocalyptic*.

15. "Apocalyptic concepts and traditions are widely used in the writing [but they are used] to present a critical discussion of already existing apocalyptic views and speculation." Helmut Koester, *History and Literature Early Christianity*, 253.

16. "Early Christian prophecy used apocalyptic patterns and language to admonish and to interpret the situations of the community." Schüssler Fiorenza, *Book of Revelation*, 169.

CHAPTER 3

1. Aune, "Apocalypse Renewed," in Barr, *Reality of Apocalypse*, 69.

2. Schaff, *Ante-Nicene Christianity*, para. 8667.

3. Schüssler Fiorenza, *Book of Revelation*, 163.

4. "John will place Isaiah's words on the lips of an angel. Thus, the boundaries between recitation and re-contextualization are somewhat blurred in Revelation." Desilva, "Socio-rhetorical Interpretation of Revelation," 90.

5. Fekkes, *Isaiah and Prophetic Traditions*.

6. Blenkinsopp, *Isaiah 1–39*, 183.

7. "Oppression always has two sides . . . [and] destroys humanity on both sides. . . . The evil the perpetrator commits robs him of his humanity, the suffering he inflicts dehumanizes the victim." Moltmann, *Experiences in Theology*, 185.

8. Bauckham, *Climax of Prophecy*, 4.

9. Blenkinsopp, *Isaiah 1–39*, 279.

10. Oswalt, *Isaiah, Chapters 1–39*, 302.

11. Blenkinsopp, *Isaiah 1–39*, 276.

12. Blenkinsopp articulates the magnitude of this imagery by arguing that the swallowing up of death is not merely an anachronistic confidence in the afterlife, but instead is reflective of a mythological tradition that "pulls the meaning of the phrase in the direction of death as something more than a punctual event, as a force of disorder, negativity, and aridity, morally and physically" (359).

13. BDAG, *Greek-English Lexicon*, 828.

14. I lifted this excellent phrase, "the anti-God powers of Sin and Death," from my friend David Harvey, who was summarizing the work of Beverly Roberts Gaventa, "Neither height nor depth: Discerning the cosmology of Romans," 265–278.

CHAPTER 4

1. Koester, *Revelation*, 96.

2. Aune, *Revelation 1–5*, 133.

3. Wright, *Revelation for Everyone*, 12.

4. Ramsay, *Letters to the Seven Churches*, 357–59.

5. Mounce, *Book of Revelation*, 94.

6. Hemer, *Letters to the Seven Churches*, 131–33.

7. Wright, *Revelation for Everyone*, 37.

8. Aune, *Revelation 1–5*, 260.

9. Wright, *Revelation for Everyone*, 37.

10. Mounce, *Book of Revelation*, 109.

11. Sölle, *Thinking about God*, 134.

CHAPTER 5

1. "Although chapter 5 is sometimes viewed as a second, future enthronement of Christ, it is more natural to suppose that John has in mind only one [story]." Beale, *Book of Revelation*, 311.

2. Jerome writes that "the beginning and ending of Ezekiel, the third of the four, are involved in so great obscurity that like the commencement of Genesis they are not studied by the Hebrews until they are thirty years old." Schaff and Wace, *Jerome*, para. 34253.

3. *Apocalypse of Abraham* 18:3–7.

4. Duguid, *Ezekiel*, 46.
5. See Aune, *Revelation 1–5*, 298, for a discussion of eyes in ancient Near Eastern literature.
6. Keener, *Revelation*, 172.
7. Josephus, *Antiquitates judaicae* 14.35; Josephus, *Bellum judaicum* 7.105.
8. Tacitus, *Annales* 15.29; Craig R. Koester, *Revelation*, 365.
9. Josephus, *Bellum judaicum* 7.71; note the presence of the term *worthy* [*axios*] in both the language of Revelation 4:11 and ascriptions of the emperors.
10. Zissos, *Companion to the Flavian Age*, 95.
11. Zissos lists several of Domitian's political victims. Zissos, *Companion to the Flavian Age*, 95.
12. Suetonius, *Domitianus* 13.2.
13. Koester provides three reasons this claim should be read with nuance: (1) precedent before Domitian; (2) lack of inscriptional evidence for Suetonius's claim; and (3) use by those attempting to flatter the emperor. Koester, *Revelation*, 366. On the other hand, Philostratus records Domitian prosecuting a magistrate just for forgetting to mention that he was a son of the goddess Minerva in a public prayer, so his eccentricities were well known. Zissos, *Companion to the Flavian Age*, 100.
14. Dio Cassius, *Roman History* 67.4.3.
15. Brian Jones, *Emperor Domitian*, 162.
16. Koester, *Revelation*, 361. Intriguingly, this imperial choir for their downtime was stationed at Smyrna, a city identified with Roman persecution in Revelation 2:10; Friesen, *Twice Neokoros*, 21; Koester, *Revelation*, 273.
17. Zissos, *Companion to the Flavian Age*, 98–99.
18. Stauffer, *Christ and the Caesars*, 149.
19. Zissos, *Companion to the Flavian Age*, 99.
20. Stauffer, *Christ and the Caesars*, 155
21. Stauffer, 187.
22. The Christian writer Prudentius describes a blood baptism in the Roman Empire. Meyer, "Mystery Religions," in Freedman, *AYBD*, 4:943.
23. Barclay, *Revelation of John*, 2:37.
24. Stauffer, *Christ and the Caesars*, 152.
25. Stauffer, 150.

26. Bauckham, *Climax of Prophecy*, 214. Cf. Caird, *Revelation of St. John*, 75.

27. Koester, *Revelation*, 335.

28. Barr, "Apocalypse as Symbolic Transformation," 41.

29. *Sphazô*: "to butcher or murder someone." BDAG, *Greek-English Lexicon*, 979.

30. *Thyô*: "to make a cultic offering, sacrifice." BDAG, *Greek-English Lexicon*, 463.

31. Cf. Johns, "Atonement and Sacrifice," in *Christ in Anabaptist Perspective*, ed. Weaver and Mast, 132.

32. "Today the words 'poor in spirit' no longer convey the sense of spiritual destitution that they were originally meant to bear. Amazingly, they have come to refer to a praiseworthy condition." Willard, *Divine Conspiracy*, 115.

33. Friesen, *Twice Neokoros*, 36–37.

CHAPTER 6

1. Louw and Nida, *Greek-English Lexicon of the New Testament: Based on Semantic Domains*, 79.35.

2. Meyers and Meyers, *Zechariah 9–14*, 133.

3. Koester, *Revelation*, 406.

4. Barclay, *Revelation of John*, 2:5.

5. "An indirect polemic against Caesar and the 'civic tradition' of their world." Reumann, *Philippians*, 374.

6. Crossan, *God and Empire*, 19.

7. "The sequential program of Rome's imperial theology [was] religion, war, victory, peace—or more briefly peace through victory." Crossan, 25.

8. "There is a causal relationship between the actions narrated in vv. 9–11 and those of vv. 6–8." Fowl, *Philippians*, 100.

9. "('Even that') would not imply purpose but specify that the extent of such strife." Beale, *Book of Revelation*, 381.

10. Aune, *Revelation 6–16*, 395.

11. "The prices in Revelation were eight to sixteen times higher than usual, rates associated with severe shortages." Koester, *Revelation*, 396; cf. Josephus, *Antiquitates judaicae* 14.28.

12. Aune, *Revelation 6–16*, 398; Mounce, *Book of Revelation*, 144.

13. Farrar, *Seekers After God*, 219.

14. Epictetus, *Diatribai (Dissertationes)* 3.13.9.

CHAPTER 7

1. Johnson sees this moment as the climax of Revelation, a chiastic structure that informs the entire letter. Johnson, *Discipleship on the Edge*, 391–96.
2. Newton, *Observations upon the Prophecies*.
3. Snobelen, "'Time and Times,'" 537–51.
4. Schmemann, "Talk of Moscow."
5. Silva, ed., *Dictionary New Testament Theology*, 1:132; Cf. Proverbs 5:4; Jeremiah 9:15; 23:15.
6. "The mishna taught that a stone sat in the Holy of Holies and it was called the foundation [*shetiyya*] rock. A Sage taught in the *Tosefta*: Why was it called *shetiyya*? It is because the world was created [*hushtat*] from it. . . . The world was created by adding matter to the center, like the formation of clumps of earth." Yoma 54b:2.
7. Yarbro Collins, *Crisis and Catharsis*, 172.
8. Yarbro Collins, 154.
9. "Injustice against scapegoats becomes a charter for an unrestrained tide of righteous wrath against their oppressors." Heim, *Saved from Sacrifice*, 264.
10. John R. Kohlenberger and William D. Mounce offer *rebel* as an alternative translation to *transgressor*. *Kohlenberger/Mounce Concise Hebrew-Aramaic Dictionary of the Old Testament*, para. 14707.
11. Green, *Gospel of Luke*, 775. See also Nolland, *Luke 18:35–24:53*, 1076; and Neyrey, *The Passion according to Luke*, 42.
12. Craig R. Koester, *Revelation and the End*, loc. 1377 [of 2865], Kindle.

CHAPTER 8

1. "Most interpreters agree that the story of the woman in 12:1–6 resembles most closely and is perhaps drawn from the myth of the birth of Apollo." Sumney, "Dragon Has Been Defeated," 104.
2. "Nero styled himself as Apollo; his image on coins bore the radiant beams from his head that were Apollo's trademark, and his admirers acclaimed him as the god." Koester, *Revelation*, 559; cf. Dio Cassius, *Roman History* 62.20.5.

3. "Several Roman emperors had identified themselves as Apollo and had given Roma the role of Leto." Sumney, "Dragon Has Been Defeated," 104.

4. "Several temples in Corinth were for the worship of Apollo, and the famous shrine at Delphi was primarily that of Apollo. The slave girl that Paul encountered in Philippi on the way to Corinth had a spirit of Python, or one inspired by Apollo." House, "Tongues and the Mystery Religions," 138.

5. Cf. Psalm 74 for the image of a divine protagonist who battles a great dragon representing the forces of chaos. Gunkel, *Creation and Chaos*, 239–50.

6. This scene is "a portrayal of Jesus' birth." Koester, *Revelation*, 546. The woman, rather than a specific reference to either Mary or Israel, is "the experience of the people of God at all times." Sumney, "Dragon Has Been Defeated," 105; cf. Boring, *Revelation*, 152.

7. Boyd, *Crucifixion of the Warrior God*, 767–68.

8. Though the name Beelzebul appears nowhere else in Jewish writing, it seems to be a colloquial reference to Satan. The fact that no one objects when Jesus clarifies by switching to the more common vernacular would appear to confirm this suspicion. Lane, *Gospel of Mark*, 141.

9. Yarbro Collins, *Mark*, 229; cf. René Girard, *I See Satan Fall*, 34.

10. The word at the start of verse 27 that links the passages indicates "a difference with or contrast to what precedes . . . on the contrary." BDAG, *Greek-English Lexicon*, 44; cf. Mark 3:27 NRSV.

11. BDAG, *Greek-English Lexicon*, 134.

CHAPTER 9

1. The seven bowls of wrath are sometimes referred to as the seven vials.

2. For a more detailed comparison of the seven seals, and trumpets and bowls, see Mclean, "Structure of the Book of Revelation," 155; and Lambrecht, "Structuration of Revelation," 87.

3. "There are a number of suggestions as to why the diadems are placed on the horns rather than on the heads of the beast. The most plausible is that his claim to authority rests on brute force." Mounce, *Book of Revelation*, 245.

4. For an excellent discussion of the beasts of Daniel and the various identification of associated empires, see Collins, *Daniel*, 298–300.

5. Julio-Claudian dynasty, 27–68 BCE: Augustus, Tiberius, Caligula, Claudius, Nero. Flavian dynasty, 68–96 BCE: Galba, Otho, Vitellius, Vespasian, Titus, Domitian.

6. Barclay, *Revelation of John*, 2:118.

7. Tacitus, *Annales* 15.44.

8. Barnes, "Legislation against the Christians."

9. Barclay, *Revelation of John*, 2:119.

10. *Sibylline Oracles* 5.470–74.

11. Augustine, *City of God*, XX.19.3.

12. Aune, *Revelation 6–16*, 727; Koester, *Revelation*, 581; Mounce, *Book of Revelation*, 318.

13. The ESV even provides a helpful footnote, stating, "Some manuscripts 616."

14. Both variant readings of the text point to Nero. For 666, see Comfort, *New Testament Text*, 847. For 616, see Aune, *Revelation 6–16*, 770–71.

15. "The juxtaposition of buying and selling with the mark of the beast refers to the fact that Roman coins normally bore the image and name of the current emperor. . . . The inability to buy or sell would then be the result of the refusal to use Roman coins." Yarbro Collins, *Crisis and Catharsis*, 126. See also Koester, *Revelation and the End*, 132; cf. 1 Timothy 6:10.

16. Walsh and Keesmaat, *Colossians Remixed*, 168.

17. The woman is an image of the economy of Rome "at the center of a great network of trade." Craig R. Koester, "Roman Slave Trade," 769.

18. Swete argues that the language employed by John refers to little more than human livestock (cf. Ezekiel 27:13; Numbers 31:35; 1 Chronicles 5:21). Swete, *Apocalypse of St. John*, 235.

19. "This is a vivid commentary on the social conditions of the day. Slave traders regarded their human cargo as so much merchandise to be auctioned off to the highest bidder. It is estimated that there were as many as 60,000,000 slaves in the Roman Empire." Mounce, *Book of Revelation*, 336.

20. See image in Koester, *Revelation*, 720.

21. Pippen, *Death and Desire*, 98. Cf. Revelation 2:20; and Huber, *Thinking and Seeing with Women*.

CHAPTER 10

1. A figurative view of "Armageddon" is apparent also from the fact that no "mountain" of Megiddo has ever existed. Beale and McDonough, "Revelation," in Beale and Carson, *New Testament Use of the Old Testament*, 1137.

2. "There is no Mt. Megiddo." Mounce, *Book of Revelation*, 302.

3. BDAG, *Greek-English Lexicon*, 132.

4. Cline, *Battles of Armageddon*, 16.

5. Cline.

6. Aune, *Revelation 6–16*, 899; Eusebius, *Onomasticon*, ed. E. Klostermann [Leipzig, 1904], 14.31; 28.26; 58.1; 70.10; 90.12; 100.10; 108.6, 13; 110.21; 116.21; 140.1.

7. Cline, *Battles of Armageddon*, 184

8. Johns, *Lamb Christology*, 184–85.

9. Caird, *Revelation of St. John*, 260.

10. "Contrast between scenes of destruction and scenes of redemption can better be understood rhetorically." Koester, *Revelation*, 768.

11. Johns, *Lamb Christology*, 183.

12. Hagner, *Matthew 1–13*, 386.

13. Sefer Zeraim, Kilaayim 3:3, 18.

14. Žižek, *Fragile Absolute*, 21–24.

15. Caird, *Revelation of St. John*, 257.

16. Ford, "Millennium," in Freedman, *AYBD*, 4:833.

17. Schaff describes Calvin's participation in the execution of Michael Servetus with far too much diplomacy. "Calvin's indirect agency, in the first, and his direct agency in the second arrest of Servetus admit of no proper justification, and are due to an excess of zeal for orthodoxy." Schaff, *Modern Christianity*, para. 36777.

18. "At its completion, there shall be elected the elect ones of righteousness from the eternal plant of righteousness, to whom shall be given sevenfold instruction concerning all his flock" (1 Enoch 93:10).

19. "The earth will also yield fruits ten thousandfold. . . . And it will happen after these things when the time of the appearance of the Anointed One has been fulfilled and he returns with glory" (2 Baruch 29:5–30:1).

20. Ford, "Millennium," in Freedman, *AYBD*, 4:832. Cf. *4 Ezra* 7:53–55. For some background, 4 Ezra, sometimes called 2 Esdras, is not in your Bible; it is an apocalyptic text written sometime in

the period close to Revelation. 4 Ezra was probably written in the second century CE, but it is attributed to the fifth-century BCE Hebrew prophet Ezra, from whom it takes its name.

21. *Apocalypse of Elijah* 5:36–39.

22. "The Revelation does not present to us the millennialism of the atheistic Greeks. . . . Stay away from such destructive teachings, which are suitable to the silliness of the Greeks." Weinrich, ed., *Revelation*, 323.

23. "Augustine spiritualized the millennium which he taught began with the incarnation of Christ and was fully realized in the earthly church." Ford, "Millennium," in Freedman, *AYBD*, 4:834.

24. "An interrogative reference to someone or something, who? which (one)? what?" BDAG, *Greek-English Lexicon*, 1006.

25. "A large net hanging vertically, with floats on the top and sinkers on the bottom, *seine, dragnet*." BDAG, *Greek-English Lexicon*, 910.

26. "A definite person or thing, *he, him, she, her, it, they, them*." BDAG, *Greek-English Lexicon*, 153.

27. I first read this treatment of the parable in Capon, *Kingdom, Grace, Judgment*, 125.

28. Weinrich, *Revelation*, 333.

CHAPTER 11

1. "The first heaven shall depart and pass away; a new heaven shall appear" (1 Enoch 91:16).

2. "I shall transform heaven and make it a blessing of light forever. I shall (also) transform the earth and make it a blessing" (1 Enoch 45:4–5; cf. 2 Esdras 7:75; 2 Baruch 32:6).

3. Twelve thousand stadia is approximately fifteen hundred miles.

4. Determining exactly what stones the Hebrew and Greek texts are identifying has proved quite difficult, but there is consensus that the reference is to Exodus. Aune, *Revelation 17–22*, 1165.

5. Gleadow, *Origin of the Zodiac*, 129–30.

6. When the walls are described in Revelation 21:13, John lists them in the order of east, then north, then south, and finally west, which seems to be an intentional contrast to the anti-clockwise nature of the zodiac.

7. Paraphrased from Watts, *The Way of Zen*, 126.

BIBLIOGRAPHY

Augustine. *City of God*. Translated by Henry Bettenson. New York: Penguin Classics, 1972.

Aune, David E. "Apocalypse Renewed: An Intertextual Reading of the Apocalypse of John." In Barr, *Reality of Apocalypse*, 43–70.

———. *Revelation 1–5*. Word Biblical Commentary 52A. Edited by Ralph P. Martin. Grand Rapids: Zondervan, 1997.

———. *Revelation 6–16*. Word Biblical Commentary 52B. Edited by Ralph P. Martin. Grand Rapids: Zondervan, 1998.

———. *Revelation 17–22*. Word Biblical Commentary 52C. Edited by Ralph P. Martin. Grand Rapids: Zondervan, 1998.

Bailie, Gil. *God's Gamble: The Gravitational Power of Crucified Love*. Kettering, OH: Angelico Press, 2016.

———. *Violence Unveiled: Humanity at the Crossroads*. New York: Crossroad Publishing, 1996.

Barclay, William. *The Revelation of John*. Vol. 2, *Chapters 6 to 22*. The New Daily Study Bible. 3rd ed. Louisville, KY: Westminster John Knox, 2004.

Barnes, Timothy D. "Legislation against the Christians." *Journal of Roman Studies* 58, no. 1–2 (1968): 32–50.

Barr, David. "The Apocalypse as Symbolic Transformation of the World: A Literary Analysis." *Interpretation* 38 (1984): 39–50.

———. "Beyond Genre: The Expectations of Apocalypse." In Barr, *Reality of Apocalypse*, 71–90.

———, ed. *The Reality of Apocalypse: Rhetoric and Politics in the Book of Revelation*. Society of Biblical Literature: Atlanta, 2006.

Bauckham, Richard. *The Climax of Prophecy: Studies on the Book of Revelation*. London: T&T Clark, 1993.

———. *The Theology of the Book of Revelation*. New Testament Theology. Cambridge: Cambridge University Press, 1993.

Beale, G. K., *The Book of Revelation: A Commentary on the Greek Text*. New International Greek Testament Commentary. Grand Rapids: Eerdmans, 1999.

Beale, G. K., and D. A. Carson, eds. *Commentary on the New Testament Use of the Old Testament*. Grand Rapids: Baker Academic, 2007.

Beale, G. K., and Sean M. McDonough. "Revelation." In Beale and Carson, *Commentary on the New Testament Use of the Old Testament*.

Beasley-Murray, George R. *John*. Word Biblical Commentary 36. Grand Rapids: Zondervan, 1999.

Beck, Robert. *Nonviolent Story: Narrative Conflict Resolution in the Gospel of Mark*. Eugene, OR: Wipf and Stock, 1996.

Beckwith, I. T. *The Apocalypse of John*. New York: Macmillan, 1922.

Betz, Hans Dieter. *A Commentary on the Sermon on the Mount, including the Sermon on the Plain: Matthew 5:3–7:27 and Luke 6:20–49*. Edited by Adela Yarbro Collins. Hermeneia: A Critical and Historical Commentary on the Bible. Minneapolis: Fortress Press, 1995.

Blenkinsopp, Joseph. *Isaiah 1–39*. The Anchor Yale Bible 19. New Haven: Yale University Press, 1974.

———. *Isaiah 40–55*. The Anchor Yale Bible 19A. New Haven: Yale University Press, 1974.

Boring, Eugene M. *Revelation*. Louisville, KY: Westminster John Knox, 2011.

Boyd, Gregory A. "Christus Victor Atonement and Girard's Scapegoat Theory." *ReKnew*, May 17, 2017, http://reknew.org/2017/05/christus-victor-atonement-girards-scapegoat-theory/.

———. *The Crucifixion of the Warrior God: Interpreting the Old Testament's Violent Portraits of God in Light of the Cross*. 2 vols. Minneapolis: Fortress Press, 2017.

Bredin, Mark. *Jesus, Revolutionary of Peace: A Nonviolent Christology in the Book of Revelation*. Milton Keynes: Paternoster, 2003.

Brown, Raymond E. *The Gospel according to John I–XII*. The Anchor Yale Bible 29. New Haven: Yale University Press, 1974.

———. *The Gospel according to John XIII–XXI*. The Anchor Yale Bible 29A. New Haven: Yale University Press, 1974.

Brueggemann, Walter. *Interpretation and Obedience*. Minneapolis: Fortress, 1991.

Burke, John P. "The Identity of the Twenty-Four Elders: A Critical Monograph." *Grace Journal* 2, no. 3 (Fall 1961).

Caird, G. B. *A Commentary on the Revelation of St. John the Divine*. Harper's New Testament Commentary. New York: Harper and Row, 1966.

Capon, Robert Farrar. *Kingdom, Grace, Judgment: Paradox, Outrage, and Vindication in the Parables of Jesus*. Grand Rapids: Eerdmans, 2002.

Cline, Eric H. *The Battles of Armageddon: Megiddo and the Jezebel Valley from the Bronze Age to the Nuclear Age*. Ann Arbor: Michigan University Press, 2002.

Collins, John J. *Daniel: A Commentary on the Book of Daniel*. Edited by Frank Moore Cross. Hermeneia: A Critical and Historical Commentary on the Bible 27. Minneapolis: Fortress Press, 1993.

———. "Introduction: Towards a Morphology of a Genre." *Semeia* 14 (1979).

———. *The Scepter and the Star: The Messiahs and the Dead Sea Scrolls and Other Ancient Literature*. New York: Doubleday, 1995.

Comfort, Philip W. *New Testament Text and Translation Commentary*. Wheaton, IL: Tyndale House, 2008.

Crossan, John Dominic. *God and Empire: Jesus against Rome, Then and Now*. New York: Harper Collins, 2007.

Danker, Frederick W., Walter Bauer, William F. Arndt, and F. Wilbur Gingrich [BDAG]. *Greek-English Lexicon of the New Testament and Other Early Christian Literature*. 3rd ed. Chicago: University of Chicago Press, 2000.

Decker, Timothy L. "'Live Long in the Land': The Covenantal Character of the Old Testament Allusions in the Message to Laodicea (Revelation 3:14–22)." *Neotestamentica* 48, no. 2 (2014).

Desilva, David A. "A Socio-rhetorical Interpretation of Revelation: A Call to Act Justly toward the Just and Judging God." *Bulletin for Biblical Research* (1999).

Desjardins, M. *Peace, Violence and the New Testament.* The Biblical Seminar 46. Sheffield, UK: Sheffield Academic, 1997.

de Villiers, Pieter G. R. "The Violence of Nonviolence in the Revelation of John." *Open Theology* 1 (2015): 189–203.

Du Mez, Kristen Kobes. *Jesus and John Wayne: How Evangelicals Corrupted a Faith and Fractured a Nation.* New York: Liveright Publishing, 2020.

Duguid, Iain M. *Ezekiel.* The NIV Application Commentary. Grand Rapids: Zondervan, 1999.

Ekblad, E. Robert. "God Is Not to Blame: The Servant's Atoning Suffering according to the LXX of Isaiah 53." In *Stricken by God?*, edited by Brad Jersak and Michael Hardin, 180–205. Grand Rapids: Eerdmans, 2007.

Farrar, Frederic William. *Seekers After God.* London: MacMillan, 1877.

Fekkes, Jan. *Isaiah and Prophetic Traditions in the Book of Revelation: Visionary Antecedents and their Development.* Sheffield, UK: JSOT Press, 1994.

Ford, J. Massyngbaerde. "Millennium." In Freedman, *Anchor Yale Bible Dictionary*, 4:832.

———. *Revelation.* The Anchor Yale Bible 38. New Haven: Yale University Press, 1974.

Fowl, Stephen E. *Philippians.* Two Horizons New Testament Commentary. Grand Rapids: Eerdmans, 2005.

Freedman, David Noel, ed. *Anchor Yale Bible Dictionary* [AYBD]. New York: Yale University, 1992.

Friesen, Steven J. "Myth and Symbolic Resistance in Revelation 13." *Journal of Biblical Literature* 123, no. 2 (2004): 281–313.

———. *Twice Neokoros: Ephesus, Asia, and the Cult of the Flavian Imperial Family.* New York: E. J. Brill, 1993.

Fuller, J. William. "I Will Not Erase His Name from The Book of Life." *Journal of the Evangelical Theological Society* 26, no. 3 (September 1983): 297–306.

Gaventa, Beverely Roberts. "Neither Height nor Depth: Discerning the Cosmology of Romans." *Scottish Journal of Theology* 64, no. 3 (2011): 265–278.

Girard, René. *I See Satan Fall Like Lightning*. Maryknoll, NY: Orbis, 2001.

Gleadow, Rupert. *The Origin of the Zodiac*. Mineola, NY: Dover Publications, 1968.

Green, Joel B. *The Gospel of Luke*. New International Commentary on the New Testament. Grand Rapids: Eerdmans, 1997.

Guelich, Robert A. *Mark 1–8:26*. Word Biblical Commentary 34A. Grand Rapids: Zondervan, 1989.

Gunkel, Hermann. *Creation and Chaos in the Primeval Era and the Eschaton: A Religio-Historical Study of Genesis 1 and Revelation 12*. Translated by K. William Whitney Jr. Grand Rapids: Eerdmans, 2006.

Guthrie, Donald. "The Lamb in the Structure of the Book of Revelation." *Vox Evangelica* 12 (1987): 64–71.

Hagner, Donald A. *Matthew 14–28*. Word Biblical Commentary 33B. Grand Rapids: Zondervan, 1995.

Hamerton-Kely, Robert, ed. *Violent Origins: Walter Burket, René Girard, and Jonathon K. Smith on Ritual Killing and Cultural Formation*. Stanford: Stanford University Press, 1987.

Hauerwas, Stanley, and Jean Vanier. *Living Gently in a Violent World: The Prophetic Witness of Weakness*. Downers Grove, IL: InterVarsity Press, 2008.

Hays, Richard B. *The Moral Vision of the New Testament: Community, Cross, New Creation; a Contemporary Introduction to New Testament Ethics*. New York: HarperOne, 1996.

Heim, S. Mark. *Saved from Sacrifice: A Theology of the Cross*. Grand Rapids: Eerdmans, 2006.

Hemer, Colin J. *The Letters to the Seven Churches of Asia in Their Local Setting*. Sheffield, UK: JSOT, 1986.

House, H. Wayne. "Tongues and the Mystery Religions of Corinth." *Bibliotheca Sacra* 140, no. 558 (April 83): 134–50.

Howard-Brook, Wes. *"Come Out My People!" God's Call Out of Empire in the Bible and Beyond*. Maryknoll, NY: Orbis Books, 2010.

Huber, Lynn R. *Thinking and Seeing with Women in Revelation*. New York: Bloomsbury, 2013.

Jauhiainen, Marko. "'Behold, I Am Coming': The Use of Zechariah in Revelation." *Tyndale Bulletin* 56, no. 1 (2005): 157–60.

Johns, Loren L. "Atonement and Sacrifice in the Book of Revelation." In *The Work of Jesus Christ in Anabaptist Perspective: Essays in Honor of J. Denny Weaver*, edited by Alain Epp Weaver and Gerald J. Mast. Telford, PA: Cascadia Publishing House, 2008.

———. *The Lamb Christology of the Apocalypse of John: An Investigation into Its Origins and Rhetorical Force*. Eugene, OR: Wipf and Stock, 2003.

Johnson, Darrell W. *Discipleship on the Edge: An Expository Journey through the Book of Revelation*. Vancouver, BC: Regent College, 2004.

Jones, Brian. *The Emperor Domitian*. New York: Routledge, 1993.

Jones, D. R. "A Fresh Interpretation of Zech. ix–xi." *Vetus Testamentum* 12 (1962).

Keener, Craig S. *Revelation*. The NIV Application Commentary, edited by Terry C. Muck. Grand Rapids: Zondervan, 2000.

Kent, Thomas L. *Interpretation and Genre: The Role of Generic Perception in the Study of Narrative Texts*. Lewisburg, PA: Bucknell University Press, 1986.

Kittel, Gerhard, ed., and Geoffrey W. Bromiley, trans. *Theological Dictionary of the New Testament*. Grand Rapids: Eerdmans, 1964.

Klassen, William. "Vengeance in the Apocalypse of John." *Catholic Biblical Quarterly* 28 (1966): 300–311.

Koch, Klaus. *The Rediscovery of Apocalyptic*. Translated by Margaret Kohl. London: SCM, 1972.

Koehler, Ludwig, Walter Baumgartner, and Johann J. Stamm. *The Hebrew and Aramaic Lexicon of the Old Testament*. Translated and edited under the supervision of Mervyn E. J. Richardson. 2 vols. Leiden, Netherlands: Brill, 2001.

Koester, Craig R. *Revelation and the End of All Things*. Grand Rapids: Eerdmans, 2001.

———. *Revelation: A New Translation with Introduction and Commentary*. Anchor Yale Bible 38A, edited by John J. Collins. New Haven: Yale University Press, 2014.

———. "Roman Slave Trade and the Critique of Babylon in Revelation 18." *Catholic Biblical Quarterly* 70, no. 4 (2008): 766–86.

Koester, Helmut. *History and Literature of Early Christianity.* Vol. 2 of *Introduction to the New Testament.* 2nd ed. New York: de Gruyter, 2000.

LaHaye, Tim, and Jerry B. Jenkins. *Left Behind: A Novel of the Earth's Last Days.* Carol Stream, IL: Tyndale, 2011. First published 1995.

Lambrecht, Jan. "A Structuration of Revelation 4, 1–22, 5." *BETL* 53 (1980): 77–104.

Lane, William L. *The Gospel of Mark.* New International Commentary on the New Testament. Grand Rapids: Eerdmans, 1974.

Levine, Amy-Jill, ed., with Maria Mayo Robbins. *A Feminist Companion to the Apocalypse of John.* London: T&T Clark, 2009.

Levine, Amy-Jill and Marc Zvi Brettler, eds. *The Jewish Annotated New Testament.* 2nd ed. New York: Oxford University Press, 2017.

Linton, Gregory L. "Reading the Apocalypse as Apocalypse: The Limits of Genre." In Barr, *Reality of Apocalypse*, 9–42.

Longman, Tremper, III. "Form Criticism, Recent Developments in Genre Theory, and the Evangelical." *Westminster Theological Journal* 47 (1985): 46–67.

Louw, Johannes P., and Eugene A. Nida, eds. *Greek-English Lexicon of the New Testament: Based on Semantic Domains.* New York: United Bible Societies, 1989.

Malina, Bruce. *On the Genre and Message of Revelation: Star Visions and Sky Journeys.* Peabody, MA: Hendrickson, 1995.

Mason, R. A. "The Relation of Zech. 9–14 to Proto Zechariah." *ZAW* 88 (1976): 227–39.

Mayo, Philip L. *Those Who Call Themselves Jews: The Church and Judaism in the Apocalypse of John.* Eugene, OR Wipf and Stock, 2006.

Mazzaferri, Frederick David. *The Genre of the Book of Revelation from a Source-critical Perspective.* Berlin: Walter de Gruyter, 1989.

McKenzie, John L. *Second Isaiah.* The Anchor Yale Bible 20. New Haven: Yale University Press, 1974.

Mclean, John A. "The Structure of the Book of Revelation and Its Implication for the Pre-Wrath Rapture." *Michigan Theological Journal* 2, no. 2 (Fall 1991).

Meyer, Marvin W. "Mystery Religions." In Freedman, *Anchor Yale Bible Dictionary*, 4:941–45.

Meyers, Carol L., and Eric M. Meyers. *Zechariah 9–14*. The Anchor Yale Bible 25C. New Haven: Yale University Press, 1974.

Moltmann, Jürgen. *Experiences in Theology: Ways and Forms of Christian Theology*. Minneapolis: Fortress Press, 2000.

Morris, Leon. *Apocalyptic*. London: Intervarsity Press, 1973.

Mounce, Robert H. *The Book of Revelation*. New International Commentary on the New Testament. Grand Rapids: Eerdmans, 1998.

Myers, Ched. *Binding the Strong Man: A Political Reading of Mark's Story of Jesus*. Maryknoll, NY: Orbis, 1988.

Nakashima Brock, Rita, *Journeys by the Heart. A Christology of Erotic Power*. New York: Crossroad, 1988.

Nakashimi Brock, Rita and Rebecca Ann Parker. *Proverbs for Ashes: Violence, Redemptive Suffering, and the Search for What Saves Us*. Boston: Beacon Press, 2001.

Newton, Isaac. *Observations upon the Prophecies of Daniel, and the Apocalypse of St. John*. First published 1733.

Neyrey, Jerome H. *The Passion according to Luke: A Redaction Study of Luke's Soteriology*. Eugene, OR: Wipf and Stock, 2007.

Nolland, John. *Luke 18:35–24:53*. Word Biblical Commentary 35C. Grand Rapids: Zondervan, 1993.

North, Robert. "Violence and the Bible: The Girard Connection." *Catholic Biblical Quarterly* 47, no. 1 (1985).

Oswalt, John. *The Book of Isaiah, Chapters 1–39*. New International Commentary on the Old Testament. Grand Rapids: Eerdmans, 1986.

Pagels, Elaine. *Revelations: Visions, Prophecy, and Politics in the Book of Revelation*. New York: Penguin, 2012.

Peterson, Eugene. *Reversed Thunder: The Revelation of John and the Praying Imagination*. San Francisco: Harper, 1988.

Pippen, Tina. *Death and Desire: The Rhetoric of Gender in the Apocalypse of John*. Eugene, OR: Wipf and Stock, 2021.

Rahner, Karl. *The Trinity*. Translated by J. Donceel. London: Bloomsbury Academic, 2001.

Ramsay, W. M. *The Letters to the Seven Churches*. London: Hodder and Stoughton, 1904.

Reumann, John. *Philippians*. The Anchor Yale Bible 33B. New Haven: Yale University Press, 1974.

Ronning, J. L. "The Targum of Isaiah and the Johannine Literature." *Westminster Theological Journal* 69, no. 2 (2007): 247–78.

Schaff, Philip. *Ante-Nicene Christianity*. Vol. 2 of *History of the Christian Church*. New York: Charles Scribner's Sons, 1910.

———. *Modern Christianity: The Swiss Reformation*. Vol. 8 of *History of the Christian Church*. New York: Charles Scribner's Sons, 1910.

Schaff, Philip, and Henry Wace, eds. *Jerome: Select Works and Letters*. A Select Library of the Nicene and Post-Nicene Fathers of the Christian Church, Second Series, 6. New York: Christian Literature Publishing, 1890.

Schick, Eduard. *The Revelation of St John*. The New Testament for Spiritual Reading 12. London: Sheed and Ward, 1977.

Schmemann, Serge. "The Talk of Moscow; Chernobyl Fallout: Apocalyptic Tale and Fear." *New York Times*, July 26, 1986, https://www.nytimes.com/1986/07/26/world/the-talk-of-moscow-chernobyl-fallout-apocalyptic-tale-and-fear.html.

Schüssler Fiorenza, Elisabeth. *The Book of Revelation: Justice and Judgment*. Minneapolis: Augsburg, 1998.

Silva, Moisés, ed. *New International Dictionary of New Testament Theology and Exegesis*. 2nd ed. Grand Rapids: Zondervan, 2014.

Snobelen, Stephen D. "'A Time and Times and the Dividing of Time': Isaac Newton, the Apocalypse, and 2060 A.D." *Canadian Journal of History* 38 (December 2003): 537–52.

Sölle, Dorothee. *Thinking about God: An Introduction to Theology*. Eugene, OR: Wipf and Stock, 2016.

Stauffer, Ethelbert. *Christ and the Caesars*. Eugene, OR: Wipf and Stock, 2008. First published 1952.

Sumney, Jerry L. "The Dragon Has Been Defeated—Revelation 12." *Review and Expositor* 98, no. 1 (Winter 2001): 103–15.

Svigel, Michael J. "Extreme Makeover: Heaven and Earth Edition—Will God Annihilate the World and Re-create It Ex Nihilo?" *Bibliotheca Sacra* 171, no. 684 (2014): 401–17.

Swete, Henry B. *The Apocalypse of St. John*. Grand Rapids: Eerdmans, 1951.

Thatcher, Tom. *Greater Than Caesar: Christology and Empire in the Fourth Gospel*. Minneapolis: Fortress Press, 2009.

Thompson, Leonard L. *Revelation*. Abingdon New Testament Commentaries. Nashville: Abingdon, 1998.

Tobin, Thomas H. "*Logos*." In Freedman, *Anchor Yale Bible Dictionary*, 4:347.

Vanhoye, Albert. *Old Testament Priests and the New Priest: According to the New Testament*. Leominster, UK: Gracewing, 2009.

Walsh, Brian J., and Sylvia Keesmaat. *Colossians Remixed: Subverting the Empire*. Downers Grove, IL InterVarsity Press, 2004.

Waltke, Bruce. *Finding the Will of God: A Pagan Notion?* Vancouver, BC: Regent College, 1995.

Watts, Alan. *The Way of Zen*. New York, Pantheon Books, 1951.

Weaver, Denny. *The Nonviolent Atonement*. Grand Rapids: Eerdmans, 2001.

Weinrich, William C., ed. *Revelation*. Ancient Christian Commentary on Scripture 12, edited by Thomas C. Oden. Downers Grove, IL InterVarsity Press, 2005.

Wendland, Ernst R. "The Hermeneutical Significance of Literary Structure in Revelation." *Neotestamentica* 48, no. 2 (2014): 447–76.

Willard, Dallas. *The Divine Conspiracy: Rediscovering Our Hidden Life in God*. San Francisco: HarperOne, 2009.

Williams, James. *The Bible, Violence, and the Sacred: Liberation from the Myth of Sanctioned Violence*. Eugene, OR: Wipf and Stock, 1991.

Wink, Walter. *Engaging the Powers. Discernment and Resistance in a World of Domination*. Minneapolis: Fortress Press, 1992.

Wright, N. T. *Revelation for Everyone*. Vol. 18 of New Testament for Everyone. Louisville, KY: Westminster John Knox, 2011.

Yarbro Collins, Adela. *The Apocalypse*. New Testament Message 22. Collegeville, MN: The Liturgical Press, 1979.

———. *The Combat Myth in the Book of Revelation*. Eugene, OR: Wipf and Stock, 1976.

———. *Crisis and Catharsis: The Power of the Apocalypse*. Philadelphia: The Westminster Press, 1984.

———. "The Early Christian Apocalypses." *Semeia* 14 (1979): 61–121.

———. *Mark: A Commentary*. Edited by Harold W. Attridge. Hermeneia: A Critical and Historical Commentary on the Bible 62. Minneapolis: Fortress Press, 2007.

———. "The Political Perspective of the Rev to John." *Journal of Biblical Literature* 96, no. 2 (1977).

Zissos, Andrew. *A Companion to the Flavian Age of Imperial Rome*. Chichester, UK Wiley-Blackwell, 2016.

Žižek, Slavoj. *The Fragile Absolute—or, Why Is the Christian Legacy Worth Fighting For?* London: Verso, 2000.